Dakota Wesleyan University:
Century I

by Violet Miller Goering

Copyright © 1996 by
Dakota Wesleyan University

Library of Congress
Catalog Card No. 96-72048

ISBN 1-57579-040-8

Pictured on the cover: Graham Hall (shown in 1982). Completed in 1904 as Century Memorial Hall, the building was renamed Graham Hall in 1910 in honor of William Graham, DWU's President from 1893-1903.

Printed in United States of America

Table of Contents

INTRODUCTION v

CENTENNIAL PERSPECTIVE vii

CHAPTER I
Steeple and Gown: 1860-1886 1

CHAPTER II
The Formative Years: 1885-1903 7

CHAPTER III
Rhetoric Becomes Reality: 1903-1930 31

CHAPTER IV
Built on a Rock: 1930-1952 49

CHAPTER V
Out of Disaster Into a New Day: 1952-1969 63

CHAPTER VI
The Quest for Excellence: 1969-1985 .89

CENTENNIAL OBSERVANCES 106

ENDNOTES 109

APPENDICES:
   A. Dakota Wesleyan University Leadership:
       Presidents 119
       Board of Trustees 119
   B. Academic Deans 120
   C. Business Managers 121
   D. Financial Overview 122
   E. Enrollment: 1885-1985 123
   F. Graduates and Majors 127
   G. Benefactors 129
   H. Distinguished Alumni 131

INDEX 137

Introduction

This brief history of Dakota Wesleyan University's first hundred years—1885 to 1985—is written with a dual purpose: first, to serve as a source of institutional information; and secondly, to provide understanding and reminiscences for the school's many friends and alumni. A conscious effort has been made to relate the development of Dakota Wesleyan University in the context of its Great Plains setting and the social and economic milieu of the times.

Coverage of the first seventy-five years is based in large part on my master's thesis, "Dakota Wesleyan University: 1885-1960" (University of South Dakota, 1970). For that sector, I am indebted to Dr. Matthew D. Smith, then President Emeritus of Dakota Wesleyan University, for his keen interest and reading of the manuscript; and to Dr. Cedric Cummins, my mentor and Head of the History Department of the University of South Dakota at that time.

Appreciation is hereby expressed to Dr. James B. Beddow for granting access to official records and editing of the manuscript; to Dr. Donald Messer and Mr. Gordon Rollins for their reading of the manuscript and contributions of vital information; and to the Wesleyan staff and alumni for providing materials and granting interviews. Thanks also to my husband, Dr. Orlando J. Goering, for his encouragement and assistance, and to DWU President Jack Ewing and Debbie Asmus, secretary, for bringing this manuscript to publication.

Violet Miller Goering

Dakota Wesleyan University

Centennial Perspective

In 1883, a small band of Methodist settlers meeting in Dakota Territory secured a charter to found a college—Dakota University. These hardy pioneers, driven by the Wesleyan mandate to join knowledge and vital piety, "built a college of stone while living in houses of sod." Two years later, President William Brush and seven faculty welcomed forty students to campus which consisted of Merrill Memorial Hall. Dakota University had moved from a dream to reality.

As we celebrate Dakota Wesleyan University's Centennial and look toward its second century of service, we are reminded of a rich heritage forged from a harsh prairie landscape. Like many small, denominational colleges planted on the frontier, Dakota Wesleyan nearly perished in its early years. In March 1888, a fire destroyed Merrill Hall. Two students died and the college hung in the balance. The Mitchell community, recognizing that the Dakota Mission Conference could offer no assistance, rallied to save the school.

Functioning primarily as a "prep school" in the early days, the college program produced only seven graduates in the first eleven years. Despite its shaky origins, the institution gained a foothold and by 1920 was the largest independent college in the state with a full-time enrollment of over 300. Dakota Wesleyan shared with the University of South Dakota the distinction of being the first college in the state accredited by the North Central Association of Colleges and Secondary Schools.

During its first 100 years, this small prairie college has displayed remarkable resiliency in the face of adversity. Heroic leadership by Earl A. Roadman carried Wesleyan through the Great Depression. Surmounting incredible odds, President Roadman and Harmon Brown kept the college alive on "tuition" in the form of corn, chickens, and livestock. When World War II depleted the student body and enrollment dropped to 165, Matthew Smith returned to his alma mater to provide fresh vision and much needed energetic leadership. Robert Wagner led the college "out of disaster into a new day" by spearheading a successful drive to raise $750,000 for a new administration building after a fire razed College Hall in 1955. In recent years, Gordon Rollins' financial stewardship has placed him in the first rank of Wesleyan giants. Dakota Wesleyan has indeed been blessed with gifted leadership at critical points in its history.

Throughout the years, Dakota Wesleyan has remained true to its mission of providing a "formative" growth experience. An unceasing succession of concerned faculty and staff have invested themselves in the lives of students in special ways. Today, all of us, faculty, staff, alumni, and friends are called upon to affirm the past and to insure that this marvelous tradition remains to serve future generations.

James B. Beddow, President
April 1985

Chapter I

Steeple and Gown: 1860-1886

Dakota Wesleyan University, located at Mitchell, South Dakota, is a co-educational liberal arts college which also offers a limited amount of vocational training. It was founded by the Dakota Conference of the Methodist Episcopal Church and in its centennial year was under the auspices of the South Dakota Conference of the United Methodist Church through its election of the members of the Board of Trustees, the institution's governing body.

Travelers on the Chicago, Milwaukee and St. Paul Railroad in the summer of 1884 found Mitchell, Dakota Territory to be a typical frontier village, its air permeated with dust and optimism. Like every other whistle stop, it aspired to being named the territorial capitol. Moreover, Mitchell was already building a university, the combined effort of local businessmen who considered it a community asset and Methodists concerned for the propagation of their faith.

The history of Dakota Wesleyan University is rooted in the efforts of the church to accompany the westward movement of the pioneer family. Typical of its vital role in the conquest of the frontier, the Methodist Church began organized work in Dakota Territory within a year after it was opened for settlement. At that time Septimus W. Ingham was appointed to minister to the spiritual needs of the scattered homesteaders in the wedge between the Missouri and Big Sioux River by the Upper Iowa Conference of the Methodist Episcopal Church at its yearly meeting in August 1860.[1]

Early growth in the new territory was stunted by drought and the growing conflict between the indigenous peoples and the newcomers; however, the influx of Methodists from eastern states kept pace with the later rapid population expansion during the years of the Dakota Boom. This caused the Church to experience phenomenal growth in the years between 1877 and 1885, transforming it from

1

a struggling mission outpost to a strong and independent institution with its own, though not yet officially adopted, college. The churches east of the Missouri River were formed into the Dakota Mission of the Methodist Episcopal Church in 1880. It was reorganized as the Dakota Conference of the Methodist Episcopal Church in 1885, signaling the coming of age of Dakota Methodism.[2]

The town of Mitchell, laid out in 1880 by the Chicago, Milwaukee and St. Paul Railroad, soon became a center of denominational activity. Former mayor Martin Osterhaus's remark that the Methodists arrived in Mitchell "two years before the 'Jim' River came through"[3] attests to their early presence in the area, predating both the coming of the railroad and the incorporation of the town. Plans to open a circuit serving Methodist worshippers in the Mitchell area were formulated in 1879. The local congregation was organized in 1881. Within two years they had constructed a house of worship and were actively promoting the erection of Dakota University.[4]

Such an avid pursuit of "schooling" had not always characterized the denomination. American Methodists had, in fact, long looked askance at higher education. "With the fox hunting parsons of colonial days still fresh in their memory, the Methodists demanded tangible evidence of conversion and dedication in their circuit riders, rather than proficiency in Latin and Greek."[5] Bishop Francis Asbury expressed relief when Cokesbury College, Methodism's first attempt at higher education in America, was reduced to ashes at the close of the eighteenth century.[6] His view that the need for primary and secondary schools was greater than the need for colleges was reiterated by the General Conference of 1840.[7]

However, as Methodism evolved from a pietistic sect serving the disinherited to an established middle class denomination, its views on higher education altered.[8] The Board of Education of the Methodist Episcopal Church took form in 1864, and the founding and development of colleges received great impetus from the Centennial Conference of 1866.[9] By the latter part of the nineteenth century, America's largest and fastest growing denomination had clasped hands with the collegiate community. Only the Baptists and Presbyterians equaled the fervor of the Methodists in the establishment of colleges.

Wesley's apostles in Dakota Territory were to be no exception. The Dakota Mission at its first annual conference in 1880 designated Cornell College at Mount Vernon, Iowa, as its educational center. Among the reasons given for Cornell's selection was its location "in the midst of a people of advanced morals," as evidenced by the absence of liquor and gambling saloons.[10] It was also the alma mater of numerous conference leaders.

Meanwhile, interest in a college within Dakota Mission was growing. At the annual meeting held in Parker in 1882, a committee of five was appointed to investigate offers of land and money and to report its findings at the next regular session. As a result of this resolution, a private group of promoters incorporated Dakota University and Dakota College Alliance (later known as Dakota Wesleyan University) on July 13, 1883, for the purpose of establishing a nonsectarian university in the city of Mitchell.[11] The incorporators[12] were all ordained Methodist ministers and included Wilmot Whitfield, Superintendent of Dakota Mission and chairman of the special investigating committee. There was, however, no close organizational tie between the proposed Dakota University and Dakota Mission.

Although not mentioned in the official record, the newly formed corporation must have been the talk over many a cup of coffee when the delegates met for the fourth annual session of the Dakota Mission assembled at Huron three months later (October 1883). After considering proposals from Huron, Mitchell and Ordway—an ambitious little town north of Aberdeen bearing the name of the territorial governor—the offers of both Mitchell and Ordway were accepted as the locations of two educational institutions. It was reasoned that the southern half of the Mission would patronize Mitchell while the northern half would give its support to Ordway. Huron was eliminated because of its close proximity to Mitchell.[13]

Accordingly, Mitchell and Ordway each proceeded with plans to build a university, Mitchell holding the lead. Dakota University entered into negotiations with A.M. Bowdle, a prominent citizen of Mitchell, in the spring of 1884, whereby lands owned by Bowdle were platted as the University Addition to the city of Mitchell. A portion was designated for the campus and the remainder divided into lots and sold at high prices, the purchasers understanding that they were making donations to the proposed institution. Construction of a university building, under the supervision of I. N. Pardee, was begun in the early summer of 1884. The cornerstone was laid by Bishop Edward G. Andrews on September 3 in an enthusiastic ceremony with the citizens of Mitchell, the band, and the fire department joining in a huge parade led by the Honorable Abner E. Hitchcock. The walls of Dakota University were under construction when Dakota Mission delegates convened at Mitchell five weeks later (October 10, 1884).[14]

This was hardly neutral ground in the incipient fight between Mitchell and Ordway over the location of the college. A motion, introduced by the Mitchell promoters, that the Mission adopt "only one institution of the higher grade" triggered a prolonged and lively discussion.[15] The Ordway contingent, led by the Reverend O. A. Phillips, staunchly opposed the proposition. "Brethren," he shouted during the heat of the debate, "if you take our school away from us, what will we do with the large basement we have already dug?" "Cut it into sections and sell it for post holes," retorted a Mitchell enthusiast as the crowd applauded.[16] Presiding Bishop Edward G. Andrews left the chair to admonish the battlers and urged them not to repeat the mistakes of their Iowa brethren by multiplying institutions: "Establish only one school, and make it a credit to Dakota Methodism." Final confrontation was postponed by giving both Ordway and Mitchell another year's time to meet their pledges of 1883. A commission was also appointed to evaluate the new offers and attend to features of the Dakota University charter that were considered objectionable by some.[17]

In accordance with the wishes of the Church, the appointed commission, in consultation with officials at Dakota University, made such revisions as were deemed necessary[18] and formed a new corporation.[19] Meanwhile, construction of Merrill Memorial Hall at Dakota University continued. William Brush was elected as the first president at a meeting of the Board of Directors held on May 23, 1885. Classes commenced that fall.

Hard times rode the plains in the mid-eighties. The great surge of new settlers which in 1882 alone had doubled the membership of Dakota Mission ebbed to a mere trickle. Such economic factors convinced many of the inadvisability of founding more than one college. The newly formed Dakota Conference of the Methodist Episcopal Church, meeting for its first session at Blunt in October, 1885, abandoned all attempts to establish Central Dakota University at Ordway and disclaimed all responsibility for the failure of the enterprise.[20]

Despite the elimination of its rival claimant, Dakota University's hopes of gaining the patronage of the Methodist Church at this session were shattered. The Conference adopted a report from the

Committee on Education which repudiated the existing corporation. It stipulated that all University lands and the University building, complete and furnished, be handed over with no outstanding debts to a new corporation, the members of which were listed by the report. Failing this "for any reason," the Conference would "make provision for the founding of a college or university elsewhere."[21]

Numerous factors influenced the denial of patronage in 1885. There appears to have been genuine hesitation due to the school's indebtedness and the fact that University lands were still in private hands. Also, though the new corporation specified a larger percentage of Methodists in its membership, it did not guarantee control by the Dakota Conference.

It is apparent that compromises were reached by the time the Conference convened at Watertown in 1886. An immediate transfer of property was not demanded. Members of the existing Board were retained and its membership enlarged. According to the by-laws as finally approved, members of the Board of Directors were to be elected by the Dakota Annual Conference. Two-thirds were to be ministers or members of the Methodist church, and a majority were to reside within the bounds of the Dakota Conference.

Assured that the Articles of Incorporation placed the control of Dakota University within the power of the Dakota Conference, the school was accepted by a unanimous and rising vote, followed by the singing of "Praise God from Whom All Blessings Flow." Among those who spoke afterward were Dr. William Brush, president of Dakota University, and I.N. Pardee, president of the Board of Directors — "when he could command his emotions."[22]

The Ordway constituency transferred its support to Dakota University. Furthermore, O.A. Phillips, who had labored so gallantly for the establishment of Central Dakota University, moved to Mitchell for his retirement. The home he built near campus was deeded to the school by his widow and, as Phillips Hall, served as a residence for students and faculty until it was dismantled in 1961.

In the years prior to 1886, Dakota University was mainly the product of an aggressive group of promoters in collaboration with the city of Mitchell. It was their intent from the beginning that Dakota University would become the official school of the Dakota Conference of the Methodist Episcopal Church. After many delays and the formation of a new corporation, the school was placed under the control of the Dakota Conference and was accepted by that body as its official education institution in 1886.

5

Chapter II

The Formative Years: 1885-1903

Administrative Highlights

Recitations mingled with the staccato rhythm of hammers when Dakota University opened its doors to approximately forty students in the late fall of 1885. It was housed in a single building, Merrill Memorial Hall, named in honor of Bishop S.M. Merrill, an influential organizer of Methodism in Dakota. The campus, consisting of twenty acres at the south edge of town, commanded "a magnificent view in all directions,"[1] as there were few houses within a half mile and the surrounding prairie was still the domain of the coyote and gopher. Merrill Hall, a Sioux quartzite[2] structure, housed dormitory rooms for students, the president's living quarters, recitation rooms, and a chapel on its three upper stories. A large dining hall was located on the first floor.

Serving as president of Dakota University was the Reverend William Brush, a co-founder of the college. His was an arduous role. As did other college presidents of the nineteenth century, he also served as bursar, chaplain, dean of students, professor of philosophy, and director of public relations, plus a variety of expected fringe activities, such as handling a student's spending money.[3] Associated with President Brush as members of the faculty were J. Shanton, Fred C. Eastman and Mrs. Eastman. Shanton left at the close of the first year. Mr. E.T. Moyer and Miss Carlotta Moyer joined the teaching staff for the second year.

Enrollment remained small, dropping to eight or ten students during the spring quarter of 1887.[4] The following fall brought an upsurge of activity, resulting in part from the support gained from the Dakota Conference of the Methodist Episcopal Church. The faculty was enlarged; enrollment passed the hundred mark; literary societies were activated, and a college paper published. Regrettably, the new burst of progress was brief.

During the bitterly cold and blustery night of March 9, 1888, fire destroyed Merrill Hall. The blaze, discovered at about three o'clock in the morning, blocked the exit of the six men rooming on the top floor. Their only escape from the holocaust was to leap from the windows to the frozen earth. Horton Pitcher and Giles W. Parkin, a ministerial student from England, died of injuries. Arza Janes and others were maimed for life. Professor Theodore A. Duncan escaped by means of a clothesline. There were no telephones, no ambulances, no hospitals. The people of Mitchell cared for the dying, nursed the injured, reimbursed student losses, and furnished the use of the Barber building downtown for the continuation of classes. The spring term opened eleven days after the fire. The first commencement exercises were held that June with four graduates: Oliver Edward Murray from the classical course; and Beulah Windle, Emily Rogers, and May Skinner from the teacher training course.

Classes resumed in the Barber building in the fall of 1888. This may well have been the most dismal year in the history of the school. Enrollment plunged. Faculty turnover was nearly complete. The curriculum was curtailed. Saddled with debts and lacking facilities, it was questionable whether Dakota University could remain operative. Furthermore, the Dakota Conference declared itself unable to assist.

Dakota University was saved at this critical juncture by the unflagging enthusiasm of President Brush and the devotion of the people of Mitchell. College Hall, erected on the foundation of Merrill Memorial Hall, welcomed the return of students to the campus in September 1889.

Faced with Dakota University's dire economic straits, President Brush spent prolonged periods of time soliciting funds in eastern states. During his absence, administrative duties fell on P.O. Reno, vice president in 1887-1888. At Reno's departure, the Board of Directors, at their annual meeting on June 27, 1888, bypassed the recommendation of the committee on the presidency to re-elect Brush for another year to spend his time in the East, "the same as last year." Instead, the Board cast a unanimous vote for A.W. Adkinson, pastor of the First Methodist Church of Mitchell, for president of Dakota University. The Board reconvened the following day, and after protracted discussion, rescinded their previous action and reelected Brush as president and Adkinson as vice president.[5] What happened in the intervening twenty-four hours is not on official record. The dissension over the election was carried to the Conference floor in October, the Bishop being requested to approve Brush and Adkinson as president and vice president.[6]

Adkinson filled the position of vice president in charge of the school for two years, assisted by T.A. Duncan, professor of mathematics, and Miss Dell Noble, preceptress and professor of history and English literature. During his first year as college administrator Adkinson was relieved of his pastoral duties and devoted his entire effort to Dakota University. He was reappointed pastor of the local congregation for 1889-1890, dividing his time between church and college. For this dual responsibility he received a thousand dollars from the church and two hundred dollars from the school. The Adkinson family lived at Dakota University, paying ten dollars a month for room and board. In the fall of 1890, Adkinson asked to be relieved of his duties at Mitchell and accepted a pastorate at Watertown.

Brush, who had been absent an entire year, was rehired in June 1890. That fall Brush accepted a political appointment by President Benjamin Harrison as United States consul to Italy and was granted a year's leave of absence. Professor Levi Asa Stout was placed in charge of the school. Restlessness over the continued absence of President Brush increased and procedures to secure a new president were begun. At the annual meeting of the Board in June 1891, Stout was named acting president and Brush was appointed financial agent of Dakota University, being assigned to raise funds outside of Dakota Conference territory to make up his own back salary. In early September, at a special meeting of the Board, Brush was elected chancellor of Dakota University with a year's leave of absence, and Charles O. Merica was named president. Brush returned from Italy the same fall. He was surprised and hurt to find himself reduced to a solicitor of funds and another man elevated to the presidency. His resignation followed shortly and he accepted the presidency of Morningside College, a Methodist school at Sioux City, Iowa.[7]

According to all testimony there was no question of President Brush's ability or of his devotion to Dakota University. He was instrumental in getting the college located in Mitchell and made it his personal concern to see it through the crucible of its early years. As a promoter and money raiser he was unsurpassed. It could be said of Brush, as it had been said of Increase Mather, an early

9

president of Harvard, that he was easily one of the most distinguished men that the college had for its president, "yet, by treating the presidency as a part-time job, he proved one of the least useful."[8]

Charles O. Merica, an ordained Methodist minister and graduate of DePauw University, assumed the presidency at the opening of the winter term in January 1892. A serious throat ailment prompted his resignation the following August (1892), and Levi Asa Stout, as acting president, again assumed the administrative role. Stout had come to Dakota University in 1888 as professor of ancient languages and principal of the Normal Department. Serious consideration was given to naming him president, but some considered him unqualified because he was not an ordained minister nor an effective speaker and could not go out into the field and "beg" money.[9] He resumed his former position on the teaching staff when William I. Graham was elected president in 1893.

It is obvious that Dakota University was undergoing an administrative crisis. Since its opening in the fall of 1885 it had not had a single administrator carrying the title of president who had both remained in residence and held the office more than a year. The administration of William I. Graham, 1893-1903, was one of stabilization. A Methodist minister and graduate of Ohio Wesleyan University, he had held several university teaching positions prior to his election as president of Dakota University. The decade of his incumbency opened with the panic of 1893. The economic depression was compounded in Dakota by drought and grasshoppers. Nonetheless, Graham succeeded in liquidating institutional debts and entered on a program of expansion. The first Conference-wide financial campaign was launched to fund the building of Century Memorial Hall. Ground-breaking ceremonies were held May 8, 1901. The building was completed in 1904. Century Memorial Hall served as a girls' dormitory, a dining hall and kitchen, a girls' gymnasium, and music studio. It was renamed Graham Hall in honor of President Graham in 1910. Graham instigated numerous curricular changes and a general upgrading of scholastic standards. Though there were no graduates from the college division between 1893 and 1897, explicable on the basis of economic stress and stiffened course requirements, statistics show the first appreciable increase in enrollment in that division during the years of Graham's administration.[10]

Agitation for change led to Graham's resignation in 1903. He remained with Dakota University another year as vice president and professor of Greek and psychology and assisted in raising the last sixty thousand dollars needed to complete Century Memorial Hall. His modest accomplishments laid the groundwork for the commendable progress of Dakota University under his successor, Thomas Nicholson.

Scholastic Program

Dakota University was established at the height of the university movement within the United States.[11] In keeping with the times, the founding fathers visualized a liberal arts college supplemented by vocational schools. Eleven areas of study were authorized in the Articles of Incorporation of 1885.[12] Some of these, such as business and teacher training, have continued throughout the century. Other departments, including the Preparatory, served a temporary need and were later discontinued. Law and medicine are among those that never took form.

The so-called regular departments of this period were the College, Preparatory and Normal. Of these, the Preparatory, providing a general high school education, was by far the largest. There was only a handful of college level students prior to Graham's administration.[13] In 1892, as an example, college students numbered seventeen; preparatory students numbered 101. Most of the students entering College Hall had studied the three R's in one-room schools with terms ranging from three to six months. Farms were labor-intensive and called for all available hands in springtime and fall for sowing and harvesting. Elementary school teachers were often young men and women recently out of grade school and without professional training. Public high schools were few and served limited areas, as there was no consolidation and attendance depended on the feet of man, horse or oxen. Preparatory studies were offered on three levels. In addition, sub-preparatory classes were organized for those who needed special help.

Early instruction on the college level was fragmentary, with only seven graduates in the first eleven years. Parallel courses of study, classical and scientific, were offered. Both were four-year courses and led to the degrees of Bachelor of Arts and Bachelor of Science respectively. The classical course included those studies traditionally considered necessary for the training of the mind and the development of a cultured person. Emphasis was on Latin, Greek, mathematics and philosophy. The scientific course placed

11

more emphasis on modern languages and science. New courses were added as they became standard curriculum content. By 1902-1903 science, sociology and American history were listed as requisites for the classical course, while Latin and Greek requirements were lessened.[14]

Laboratory courses became standard with the advent of modern science, but cost made well-equipped laboratories prohibitive. Dakota University's science cabinet consisted of collections of fungi, sea shells, minerals, et cetera and had little utility for modern scientific research.

The Normal Department received great impetus from the demand for teachers throughout the newly settled territory. Its basic curriculum was formed by the Territorial Board of Education (State Board of Education following statehood in 1889). Territorial (State) teaching certificates were granted on the completion of the one-year course. Beginning in 1892, teacher trainees had to meet requirements set by Dakota University in addition to state standards. A four-year course designed for those who planned to teach in high school or college was introduced in 1895 and qualified students for a bachelor's degree.[15]

The so-called special departments at Dakota University were commerce, music, art, and elocution. Studies for these disciplines were loosely structured and often offered on an individual basis. Two-year and four-year courses gradually evolved. The commerce department, organized by J. Shanton during the first school year, was the only one of the special departments to be continued at the Barber building after the fire of 1888. It was headed by M. A. Shurtleff from 1891 to 1903. There was a strong demand for individuals trained in business skills and graduates readily found employment.

Maggie Currens and Myrtle Ray Lee, sequentially, presided over the music department throughout most of this period. Teacher personnel in the art department shifted frequently until Esther Starr joined the staff in 1897. Speech training was centered in the department of elocution, headed by Augusta L. Chandler from 1889 to 1893. Interest in elocution peaked in the mid-nineties and thereafter followed the national downward trend.

Dakota University appears to have been striving for approval by the University Senate of the Board of Education of the Methodist Episcopal Church as early as 1894.[16] The University Senate, the first national standardizing agency, sought the strengthening of ties among Methodist educational institutions and elimination of spurious education. To be approved, schools were required to conform to standards set by the University Senate. Such standardization was of special benefit to small and newly organized schools such as Dakota University, as it enabled them to receive recognition with established institutions. Approved schools were also eligible for student loan funds.[17]

Most of the instructors at Dakota University were Methodist ministers. Those teaching on the college level generally were college graduates and frequently had master's degrees. The latter, however, were commonly conferred on alumni by many schools and did not carry the meaning they were to have later. Earned doctorates, a German importation, were still relatively rare. Only one is listed for this period.[18] An impoverished frontier college, Dakota University was in no position to draw educators of renown, yet student testimony abounds that it had its quota of dedicated and effective teachers. One of the first and foremost was Levi Asa Stout, who nurtured the minds and lives of Wesleyan youth for thirty-five years:

> ...a bantam physically but heavyweight where it counted most, and dedicated....He reveled in "Math," did Greek well and directed the Normal Teacher training to which he was born. He never spared the lash on the idlers and slovenly....He stands in the Wesleyan book of remembrance as a pillar of strength through critical years of the young university.[19]

Textbook assignments and classroom recitations constituted the standard means of instruction. Method as well as teaching load is indicated by the notation that Professor Stout heard an average of thirty-two recitations per week.[20] A written examination at the end of the term was customary. Candidates for graduation were examined by a visiting committee of Methodist ministers appointed by the Dakota Conference.

Student Life and Organizations

An alumnus of the early years recalled that "life in the college was more of a domestic than collegiate nature. We were a big family with venerable Dr. Wm. Brush as the paterfamilia."[21] College Hall, the sole building for nearly two decades, was a true campus center. Here the president, members of the faculty, and scholars ate their meals, conjugated Latin and dreamt their dreams. The large number engaged in high school studies created a fairly young student generation with ages ranging from fourteen to over thirty years. Occasionally in those first years when there were no organized sports the aisles doubled as a roller skating rink. The heating system was not always equal to the rigors of Dakota winters. Graduates took with them memories of shivering around chapel radiators or retreating to the engine room "as the only warm place available to the D.U. student in this life."[22] Literary societies at times called upon the president to mediate in the fight over a coveted, dingy kerosene lamp, and chickens were known to crow the matins in the women's dormitory wing.

Student rooms, furnished with bedsteads, chairs, table, washstands, pitcher, mirror, and a wardrobe for clothes, provided all the comforts of home. Occupants provided pillows, linens, a lamp and oil, napkins, and napkin rings. Growth of the student body eventually made it necessary to assign all rooms in College Hall to the ladies. The young men roomed in nearby cottages with such memorable names as Saints' Rest, White House, and Buzzards' Roost. Some family homes also kept roomers. Meals were usually taken in the college dining room in the basement of old College Hall. Grace preceded meals, and waiting on tables was done by students earning their board. Students outside the girls' dormitory enjoyed considerable freedom. There were no supervised study rooms or hours. Students were free to study in the library or chapel or to go home between classes. Afternoons provided free time for games, shopping, et cetera. Recitations were held on Saturdays instead of Mondays to discourage Sunday studying.[23]

Lack of radio, television, and commercial entertainment was no handicap to either fun or romance. There were corn poppings, candy pulls, and games at homes and at the University parlors. The outdoors offered ice skating on the "Jim" River and horse and buggy racing down dusty lanes. Although dancing was off limits, it was customary to set the chairs aside after literary society sessions for the "grand march." The first Washington Birthday Banquet was held in 1896. The most memorable item of the evening for Madge Corwin Chapman was the dessert "—seldom seen and never before tasted by many—a banana!"[24] This annual deluxe event called for a young man's best (or only) suit and derby hat, his head held high by a rigid celluloid shirt collar as he escorted his lady, attired in a lovely gown with trailing skirts.

McKinley and Bryan clubs flourished during the presidential campaign of 1896 and "two buggy loads of 'Sixteen to One' persuasion made the hard night trip to Salem to hear the silver-tongued prophet of Democracy."[25] Sickness made its rounds. An outbreak of smallpox in the spring of 1902 disrupted the athletic meet and commencement programs, and the "pest house," an isolation cottage near the observatory, became a spot to avoid. Now and then, all hands united to provide some needed facility. When President Brush secured a carload of lumber, everyone from president to subprep grabbed hammer and nails to build a boardwalk connecting the campus and the town. Builders turned pranksters on Halloween nights, carrying off sections of the walk.

Classwork was a challenge for some, a bother for others. Badger Clark, a Methodist minister's son who later became South Dakota poet laureate, attended Dakota University in 1902. "I studied out the year and got something," he wrote to a friend, "though not much, for I had no idea what I wanted." He subsequently joined an adventure party going to Cuba.[26] For one who had such a short stay, Badger Clark cast a rather long shadow. This young man, who went AWOL from chapel, was later awarded an honorary degree. He also had a library collection, a memorial scholarship, and an alumni medal established in his name.

In contrast, Byron A. Bobb, who became a medical practitioner in Mitchell for over fifty years, sold papers, walked home eight miles every weekend, and even recalled living in an old cow shed near the college where he used to cook a big bowl of oatmeal—all this for a "sheepskin." After graduating from Northwestern Medical School, Dr. Bobb returned to Mitchell, making his calls on bicycle. By 1901 he was the owner of the town's first car. On May 8 of that year, as ground-breaking ceremonies for Century Memorial Hall were in progress, Dr. Bobb roared across the campus with his new locomobile with a steam gauge blown out. In his words—

> There stood Dr. Graham ready to start the ceremony of plowing the first furrow; there wasn't a soul there—they were all around my steaming locomobile.[27]

Despite such shenanigans, the life of a preppie at Dakota University was centered on studies and graduation. Commencement activities lasted an entire week, opening formally with a joint meeting of the literary societies. Student recitals were presented by the departments of elocution and music. A field day, sponsored by the athletic association, and class day programs were added to the festivities by 1897. Baccalaureate services were held at the First

15

Methodist Church on Sunday morning, followed by a meeting of the Young Men's Christian Association (YMCA) and the Young Women's Christian Association (YWCA) on Sunday afternoon. The graduates of 1897 were the first to wear caps and gowns. The final event of the week was the annual meeting of the Board of Directors of Dakota University.

Many activities on both sides of the classroom door which are now an integral part of higher education were initiated by the students. Athletics, so liberally subsidized by colleges and universities, grew out of the spontaneous games of the young. Before the day of counselors and campus ministries, student members of the YMCA and the YWCA sought out the lonely, the bewildered, the indigent. Speech, debate, and drama were cradled in the once highly popular literary societies. These groups contributed some of the most fascinating chapters in Dakota Wesleyan University's past.

Foremost among student organizations at Dakota University were the literary societies. The Alethean Society for ladies and the Phreno Cosmian Society for men were merged into one bearing the name Phreno Cosmian following the fire of 1888. Its membership grew rapidly and in 1890 it was divided, not on the basis of sex as previously, but by the choosing of sides, as in a spelling bee, forming the Zeta Alpha and the Protonian societies. In the fall of 1897 the college classes formed the Delta Upsilon society, leaving the Zetas and Tonys, as they were commonly called, to the preparatory and special course students. They met their demise in 1903 when mixed societies were banned and were replaced by the Amphyction (boys) and Clionian (girls) societies. The Adelphian (boys) and Athenian (girls) were added soon after. College societies existent in 1903 included the Kappa Pi Phi and Daedalian for men and the Philomathean and Thalian for women. All students were required to unite with a society until 1892.

In addition to their weekly literary programs, the societies vied with each other in debate and oratory. Winners of these hotly contested competitions represented the college at intercollegiate meets. The South Dakota Intercollegiate Oratorical Society was organized in 1887 with the following members: the State Agricultural College (Brookings), the University of Dakota (Vermillion), Dakota University (Mitchell), Yankton College and Sioux Falls College. Special trains carried students to these events where they formed a cheering section for their representatives. Dakota University did not participate in the first contest held in 1888. When the contestants from Mitchell arrived at Sioux Falls for the second annual competition in 1889 they found their rivals displaying school colors. Dakota University had no colors, so its orators huddled briefly, hurried to a nearby store, and rejoined the meet festooned in blue and white ribbons.[28] Blue and white were adopted as the official school colors in 1902, winning over the "athletic" contenders, black and orange.

Assisted by such dynamic advisors as Jesse Brumbaugh and James Lawrence Lardner, Dakota University students soon proved that no one could outtalk the Methodists. An engraved chalcedony slab was to become the permanent possession of the school with the most wins in five years. Wesleyan's first school yell burst upon the world in celebration of A. C. Shepherd's victory in 1891. Dakota University eventually lost the plaque to Yankton College but was successful in winning the next award—a silver loving cup to be kept as a trophy by the school that first scored three top ratings. When E. T. Colton, Sr. returned from Brookings with the silver cup in 1898, students and city residents met him at the railroad station. He was hoisted into a new carriage decorated in blue and white and drawn by thirty college footmen. The silver cup was placed on the front seat; Mr. Colton sat on the rear seat. A band led the procession from the depot to the Mitchell Hotel. There, on a platform especially constructed for the occasion, the town's foremost citizens lauded the victor and the coeds cheered.[29] The first woman to get top honors at the state oratorical contest was Dakota University's Winifred McVay in the year 1897.

Though lacking the luster of the literary societies, Dakota University's religious organizations excelled them in outreach. A chapter of the Young Men's Christian Association was organized in 1890 with Henry Bowles as the first president. The Young Women's Christian Association was formed during the same school term. After several discouraging years, the YMCA grew to be one of the strongest factors in college life under the leadership of Ethan T. Colton and J. P. Hauser. Both associations joined the state and national YMCA-YWCA Student Movement and sent their first delegate, J. P. Hauser, to the annual student conference at Lake Geneva, Wisconsin in the summer of 1896.[30] In addition to midweek prayer meetings and a united service of song and Bible study on Sunday afternoons, the "Y"s sponsored various social and recreational activities, including the annual reception at the opening of the school year. Many University "Y" members left student ranks to become ministers and missionaries, and a few made the YMCA their life career. College students were solicited for membership in the downtown Epworth League and participated in their Sunday evening gatherings. Church and school also united for evangelistic services, and superintendents of the Mitchell district frequently included the number of college youth who had "stood up" during revival week in their annual report to the Dakota Conference. Student activities, however, were by no means limited to study and prayer. There was also time for play.

Few aspects of college and university life have undergone more dramatic change in the past hundred years than the role of sports. Athletics played a minor role at Dakota University. Sports were, at best, tolerated in the administration's educational concept. Demands on the school's budget were legion. There were no game schedules, no stipends for valuable players. Sports were of an impromptu nature, with students testing their brawn on the baseball diamond after classes. The financial situation eased after the introduction of gate receipts. Extra-mural baseball games were popular and well-contested. The first athletic event between two South Dakota colleges was a game ending in a draw between Redfield College and Dakota University in 1893. Baseball declined in popularity when track came in. Faculty and students had equal representation on the board of the Dakota University Athletic Association, organized in 1897. Prior to the formation of the Young Women's Athletic Association, the YWCA's committee on physical culture organized such games as girls' basketball and indoor baseball.

The South Dakota Intercollegiate Athletic Association was reorganized in 1894 by representatives from Vermillion, Yankton, and Sioux Falls. Mitchell was voted in at the same meeting.[31] The annual spring track meet, which included bicycle racing, was scheduled for Mitchell in 1897. It fell to the students to grade and fence a quarter-mile track and playing field, build a grandstand to seat three hundred, and make provisions for dressing rooms. Mitchell's sports-minded business and professional men contributed most of the money. Professor Theodore Duncan, business agent for the college, procured the lumber from a Minnesota company at a minimal price and the railroad delivered it at a cut rate. Classes were dismissed for a day to nail the fence. The small frame "gym" was equipped with a single shower operated by a pull cord which released a cold spray of rainwater gathered in an overhead tank.

The grandstand was built against the back of the gym. "The total undertaking was the proud campus achievement of the year...a product of school loyalty, college spirit and teamwork."[32] The facilities were acclaimed the best in the state, and Mitchell became the "permanent" location for the intercollegiate track meets.

Dakota University's showing in track tended to be mediocre, but the college responded enthusiastically to football. American football made its national debut in 1869 and spread from campus to campus with epidemic speed. Its patron saint at Dakota University was Jesse Brumbaugh.

> The tall gaunt Hoosier brought other potent ferments that he had no reserve about planting in areas where student life had gone somewhat stale. He led off in English with a vengeance. He communicated zeal for mastering his assignments that brought him up in court at faculty meetings charged with next to monopolizing the time and application of his students. Speech and forensics rose to a level that continues to distinguish Wesleyan...[33]

Brumbaugh persuaded a reluctant faculty to permit football and tutored the players. A gridiron team was organized in December 1896. The only game of that season was a skirmish with Mitchell High School on the cornfield stubbles in front of College Hall. The team's first game with another college was on November 15, 1897. It ended with a score of 40-12 in favor of Yankton College. Dakota University countered by winning the state championship in 1898, beating both the Yankton and Sioux Falls College teams. The first regular coach, P. L. Blodgett, instructor in history and political science, was appointed in 1899. The year 1901 was an all-win season (6-0) with D. B. Cropp, professor of sociology and physical director, as coach.[34]

Enthusiasm for football was mingled with ridicule and protestations of brutality. President Graham so impressed a star player of the physical hazards of the game that he took out a five hundred dollar life insurance policy to protect the Educational Board's loan to him.[35] A petition signed by fifty-two students protested the scheduling of a game on Thanksgiving Day in 1901. The petitioners objected to "'Thanksgiving football' as a sport too all-absorbing to both the participants and spectators to be conducive to the spirit of thankfulness and devotion." The faculty granted them a sympathetic ear, but the game remained scheduled.[36]

Classwork in the gymnasium became mandatory for all students at the turn of the century. This necessitated the expansion of facilities in the little frame gym and provisions for a girls' gymnasium in Century Memorial Hall. The teaching staff now included a physical director, and the faculty pondered scholastic standards for those in athletic contests. Athletics had climbed into the ivory tower through the back window. It was now an integral part of the educational program.

Several other campus organizations of these early years deserve mention. The largest, the Student Association, was composed of all students associated with the literary societies. It took charge of all matters pertaining to the student body as a whole, sponsored an annual banquet, selected the staff of editors for the student newspaper, and chose the contestants for the local oratorical contest. Class organizations existed on all preparatory and college levels and junior and senior normal classes.

A student newspaper, the *Phreno Cosmian*, was published in the fall of 1890. It had been preceded by the *University Herald*, a small news sheet issued intermittently. A. C. Shepherd, F. H. Clark, and W. S. Shepherd each served one term as editor-in-chief of the *Phreno Cosmian* in its first year. The early issues bore more resemblance to a literary magazine than to a newspaper. Prime space was devoted to essays by students and members of the faculty, poetry, and such features as translations from the classics. Jottings on campus happenings, reports of student organizations, and other miscellany were relegated to the back pages. There was no sports page. The first college annual, the *Tumbleweed*, was published in the spring of 1901 with Lauritz Miller as editor.

The Alumni Association was organized in 1888 by the first graduating class, with O. E. Murray as president. The College Alumni Association, restricted to graduates from the college department, was formed in 1898, with E. T. Colton as president. The two associations joined in an annual banquet for all graduates and members.

The élan displayed in the student organizations of this period attests to a splendid group of young people and mentors. It also points to a by-gone day antedating the intrusion of commercial entertainment and the mobility of cars. There is, after all, a limit to how far one can go on foot or by horse looking for something better to do on a cold Dakota winter's night. Neither did the weekly programs of the Zetas and Tonys compete with prime-time television or video games. Dakota University was a social and spiritual community to a degree that is difficult to duplicate on today's more cosmopolitan campuses.

Financial Overview and Summary

A solid fiscal base is essential to the survival and function of any institution. Throughout the first decade, Dakota University's existence was in jeopardy and its functions severely hampered by economic stringencies. Initially several quarters of land had been offered if the Methodists would build their school at Mitchell; however, no funds had been raised for their purchase. The amount promised was eventually reduced to one quarter and 399 feet of another quarter owned by A. M. Bowdle.[37] The school's resources consisted of profit from this real estate, cash gifts and subscriptions, and the donated labor and goods of its many friends. The largest single gift in these twenty years was a donation of $5,000 by U. S. Senator Leland Stanford of California for the rebuilding of Merrill Memorial Hall.[38] State aid was given to the normal department in the form of appropriations for students enrolled in teacher training.[39] The Conference Committee on Education regularly asked for $3,000 annually in church collections for Dakota University on University Sunday, but receipts show only half that amount at best.

At the time Dakota University was granted church patronage, it had an alleged balance of indebtedness of $2,000.[40] College and Conference were dismayed to find an accrued indebtedness of $35,000 after the fire of 1888. Insurance on Merrill Hall amounted to $5,000, leaving a deficit of $30,000.[41] The citizens of Mitchell and those interested in rebuilding raised a sum of $39,000 to liquidate the debt and secure title to the campus and unsold lots. They also erected and furnished a new building. These requirements were imposed upon them by the patronizing Conference as a condition of retaining the college.[42]

Dakota University's fiscal condition remained critical until the late nineties. At that time the Conference Committee on Education observed that "our college is no longer an experiment, but has demonstrated its right to live and to command the respect of Dakota Methodism."[43] Dakota University was made the special beneficiary of the Conference's Twentieth Century Campaign, a sum of

$35,000 for buildings and equipment, initiating the campaign to fund Century Memorial Hall.

Securing title to the land accepted by Dakota University proved problematic. Mr. Bowdle, who had entered into an agreement to sell with Dakota University and College Alliance, the first corporation, continued to hold title as trustee for the portion of land that had not been transferred to other parties until 1889, when he received final payment from Dakota University, the second corporation. Although it was understood by all that the second corporation was a continuation of the first, no formal transfer of property was made. This oversight resulted in a legal tangle when McKendree Tooke, a member of both corporations, filed suit against Dakota University in the name of the defunct Dakota Alliance, alleging that the holdings of the second corporation were illegal and Bowdle's agreement with Dakota University was void. The matter was finally resolved when Judge Frank Smith of the Circuit Court, Davison County, handed down a decision in favor of Dakota University. "Thus, in 1904, twenty years after the cornerstone laying of the first building, Dakota University had finally confirmed legal ownership of its property."[44]

Students attending Dakota University, drawn almost exclusively from the east river counties of South Dakota, shared the impoverishment of their alma mater. Committed to the principle of making educational opportunities available to as many as possible, student expenses were held to a minimum. Those unable to meet even these low costs were assisted in securing part-time employment and obtaining loans from the Methodist Board of Education. College tuition averaged eight dollars per term. Dormitory rooms rented for four dollars per term plus fifty cents per week when heated. Meals at the dining hall cost two dollars a week. The total average cost for a year was $128.

Administrative and faculty salaries were also minimal. President Brush was elected at a salary of one thousand dollars per annum plus a 10 percent commission on cash donations solicited by him. Levi Asa Stout received three hundred dollars annually and furnished rooms when he joined the teaching staff in 1888. Nine years later he was given a five-year contract of one thousand dollars per year. This was probably a top teaching salary. Individuals meriting recognition for their efforts to keep the school solvent include President Brush and T. A. Duncan. Duncan, a nephew to President Brush, assumed the difficult task of meeting expenses and satisfying creditors with a depleted treasury for many years. He superintended the building of College Hall, giving freely of his time and money, and assisted students in financial need.

The years 1885 to 1903, characterized by struggle and small beginnings, form a distinct period in the history of Dakota Wesleyan University. These are the years that saw the school established and set the patterns for the future. After a prolonged initial struggle, Dakota University achieved a fair measure of financial stability. A full course of study was implemented on both the preparatory and college levels. It is an era set apart from the years that follow by its adherence to the tradition of humanism. A new name and a new emphasis would come with the next administration.

Presidents of Dakota Wesleyan University

William Brush
1885-1891

Charles O. Merica
1891-1892

William Graham
1893-1903

Thomas Nicholson
1903-1908

Samuel Kerfoot
1908-1912

William G. Seaman
1912-1916

W. D. Schermerhorn
1917-1922

Edward D. Kohlstedt
1922-1927

Earl A. Roadman
1927-1936

Leon C. Sweetland
1936-1937

Joseph H. Edge
1937-1946

Samuel Hilburn
1946-1951

Matthew D. Smith
1952-1958

Jack J. Early
1958-1969

Robert R. Huddleston
1969-1971

Robert H. Wagner
(Interim) 1971

Donald E. Messer
1971-1981

James B. Beddow
1981-1994

An artist's rendering of Merrill Memorial Hall, built in 1885 and named after Bishop S. M. Merrill, an influential organizer of Dakota Methodism. Merrill Memorial Hall was destroyed by fire on March 9, 1888, and two students perished in the blaze.

Ground-breaking ceremonies for Century Memorial Hall in 1901. Madge Corwin is speaking in the photo.

Prexy Lodge (later renamed Music Hall), built in 1906 at the request of Dr. Thomas Nicholson to serve as a home for DWU's President. The bay window and lower porch railing were removed in the mid-1950s.

The DWU band in 1907-08.

Science Hall, built in 1912 to provide DWU students with science laboratories and classrooms. The upper stories housed the School of Music and a new chapel. Laboratories and offices were renovated in 1960.

A scene from the 1912 faculty-senior baseball game. Science Hall and College Hall are pictured.

Festivities at DWU's first Blue and White Day in 1914.

Morrow Gymnasium, built in 1919, contained the state's first indoor swimming pool, an indoor track, and a wood-floored court for intramural and recreational basketball and volleyball. The small wing at left is Stout Hall, a dormitory added in 1925 to house male students.

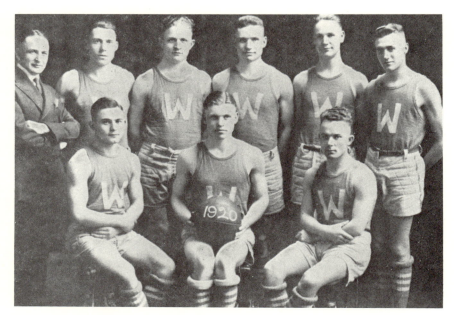

The 1920 DWU basketball team. Seated (left to right) are Eldon Link, Captain Harold Grundland, and Senn Slemmons. Standing are Coach Richard (Bud) Dougherty, Donald McPherson, Leo Harmon, Kenneth Harkness, Clarence Bruce, and Harold Wadsworth.

DWU men in uniform in 1942.

Chapter III

Rhetoric Becomes Reality: 1903-1930

Administrative Highlights

South Dakota entered the twentieth century on the upbeat. The recession of the nineties had ended, crop conditions had improved, and railroad construction tied Rapid City to the Missouri River towns of Pierre and Chamberlain by 1905-1907. The steel tracks brought homesteaders and barbed wire fences, closing the era of the open range. In addition, over four million acres of Indian reservation "surplus lands" were made available to white settlers between 1904 and 1913. Frontier towns, soddies, and tar paper shanties dotted the treeless plains. According to federal census figures, population in the western half of South Dakota grew from 43,782 in 1900 to 137,687 in 1910.

This was the Progressive Era, not only in national and state politics, but also in a general well-being that spurred institutional growth. Enrollment at Dakota Wesleyan surged; its educational program was expanded and its physical plant enlarged. This was also an era of conflict. Winds of change swept across the nation's campuses as the old goals of classical education gave way to the new trends toward pragmatism and the scientific method. Caught in the eye of the storm, college presidents lost their seats as in a game of musical chairs. At Dakota University, Thomas Nicholson took over the reins of administration from William Graham, ushering in a period of development that continued to the outbreak of World War I.

Thomas Nicholson, a graduate of Garrett Biblical Institute and Northwestern University, taught at Cornell College prior to his election as president of Dakota University in 1903. Changes followed in rapid succession. A new institutional name, Dakota Wesleyan University, was adopted in June 1904 by action of the Board of Direc-

31

tors. This ended the confusion between the college at Mitchell and the University of Dakota at Vermillion. The number of directors was increased from a maximum of fifteen to thirty-six at the same session.[1]

The official patronage of Dakota Wesleyan University, previously limited to the Dakota Conference (east river area), became statewide in 1905 when the Black Hills Mission (west river area) named Dakota Wesleyan as its college.[2] This action was the consequence of the failure of Black Hills College at Hot Springs. Chartered under Methodist auspices in 1887, Black Hills College closed its doors in 1900, a casualty of the depression of the 1890s.[3] Dakota Wesleyan now became the official and only college within the state affiliated with the Methodist Episcopal Church.

Campus changes during Nicholson's tenure included the completion of Century Memorial Hall (later Graham Hall), the relocation of the athletic grounds to the south end of the campus, and the construction of a new residence for the president. Prexy Lodge was built by the Methodists of the state at Nicholson's behest in the summer of 1906. It was home to six presidential families before being renovated as Music Hall in 1936.

There were also changes within the student body. Enrollment on the college level doubled during Nicholson's incumbency. This increase in students was accompanied by additions in the teaching staff, including men of exceptional ability who established long tenures. Among these were Samuel Weir, vice president and professor of psychology and philosophy; J. L. Seaton, professor of languages; Clarence V. Gilliland, dean of the college and professor of history; S. D. van Benthysen, dean of the School of Commerce; and Emory Wilberforce Hobson, dean of the School of Music. Whereas Dakota University had been chiefly a secondary school in enrollment and service, Dakota Wesleyan University became a full-fledged college. Major reorganizations begun in 1905 established various auxiliary departments as separate schools, giving outward form to the founding fathers' dream of a university structure.

Nicholson's administration was a period of salutary growth. He resigned in 1908 to become secretary of the Board of Education of the Methodist Episcopal Church and was elected bishop in 1916, an office he retained until his retirement at age seventy. John Prince Jenkins served as acting president during the interim between President Nicholson's departure in the spring of 1912 and President-elect Samuel Fletcher Kerfoot's arrival that fall.

Samuel Fletcher Kerfoot, a graduate of Drew Theological Seminary, was serving as superintendent of the Mankato (Minnesota) District at the time of his call to Mitchell. The monumental achievement of Kerfoot's administration was the raising of a quarter-million dollars for new buildings and additional endowment. The Conference readily approved these plans for the quarter-centennial anniversary in 1910. Of the total amount, $100,000 was used for the construction of Science Hall. The cornerstone of the large, four-story quartzite building was laid on August 1, 1911. Dedication ceremonies marking its completion were held June 5, 1912.

Science Hall provided much-needed space and facilities. The labs so essential for the popular new science courses had been virtually non-existent. Now, instead of three or four "little cooped up laboratories in the basement of College Hall," Dakota Wesleyan's science department could boast of laboratories and classrooms spread over two entire floors.[4] Supervising the budding scientists was Dr. Hilton Ira Jones, head of the department of science from 1912 to 1918. The upper stories of Science Hall housed the School of Music and a new chapel. The old chapel space at College Hall was remodeled for library use.

Kerfoot resigned in 1912 to accept the presidency of his alma mater, Hamline University. He was succeeded by Walter Grant Seaman. Seaman held a doctorate from Boston University and was professor of philosophy at DePauw University at the time of his election as president of Dakota Wesleyan.

The completion of Science Hall provided for the college's most pressing spatial needs. President Seaman was therefore in a position to bend his scholarly mind toward the improvement of the educational program. For several years, Dakota Wesleyan had been the only independent college in the state that was a member of the North Central Association of Colleges and Secondary Schools. However, in 1914 Wesleyan was dropped for lack of endowment and library facilities. A campaign for increased endowment was promptly launched. The school year of 1914-1915 was declared library year. It was appropriately marked by the hiring of the first trained and full-time librarian. The cataloging of books under the Dewey decimal system, begun in 1906, was completed. Dakota Wesleyan University was reinstated as a member of the North Central Association in 1916.

Changes were made in the qualifications for members of the Board of Directors at this time. Specific factors of church affilia-

33

tion, area of residence, and minimal percentage of clerics were eliminated. The revised by-laws simply stated that the Board of Directors should annually nominate "persons suitable to fill vacancies in its membership." Nominees were officially elected by the Dakota Conference, as before.[5] Ex-officio members of the Board included the president of the University, the resident bishop of the Methodist Church of the area, and the five district superintendents of the Dakota Annual Conference.

Meanwhile, storm clouds were gathering over Europe and within President Seaman's administration. Personal friction between two of the most competent and loyal professors caused internal divisions from which the president could not emerge unscathed. The dismissal of Samuel Weir in the spring of 1914 "in the interest of harmony and the highest good of the institution"[6] brought a torrent of protests. Many disaffected factions appeared. Student opposition was reportedly centered in the Cosmo Club, a rooming and boarding house for young men at the college with a high percentage of athletes in its membership,[7] and appears to have hinged in part on dissatisfaction with student discipline policies. In May 1916 the Executive Committee and resident directors of Dakota Wesleyan met to consider a petition signed by over two hundred students asking for Seaman's removal from the presidency.[8] His resignation was accepted at the annual meeting of the Board of Directors in June.

Although the circumstances of President Seaman's departure were regrettable, he left a notable imprint on Wesleyan's educational program. Numerous salutary changes which he sought, including the establishment of student self-government, were put into effect. Clarence V. Gilliland, dean of the college and professor of history, was named acting president and presided over the divided house until W. D. Schermerhorn took office on June 1, 1917.

President Schermerhorn, a graduate of Chicago University and Garrett Biblical Institute, had made his acceptance of the presidency contingent on two conditions, namely that he be given a five-year contract, and that the Board agree to the completion of the campaign initiated by Seaman to raise the endowment to the half-million mark.

Schermerhorn was president during World War I and the early post-war years. Meatless and wheatless days and inflation followed the United States' entrance into the war. The basement of Science Hall was temporarily converted into barracks for the campus Student Army Training Corps, mess was served at Graham Hall, and German was expunged from the curriculum. Induction of young men into military service made deep inroads on student enrollment, especially among upperclassmen, prompting President Schermerhorn's rueful observation: "The Army and the influenza almost broke up our school work."[9] One hundred seventeen faculty members and students entered military service. Fourteen of these gave their lives in the war to end all wars.

Despite the erosion of war and inflation, Dakota Wesleyan moved forward. A jubilee campaign for $400,000 for endowment was completed. Morrow Gymnasium was ready for use in 1919-1920. It boasted an indoor track and the state's first indoor swimming pool. The project was underwritten by Joseph T. and Florence Morrow, Methodists of Mitchell. A central heating plant was added to the gymnasium the same year.

Schermerhorn enjoyed general popularity and was an apt administrator. Nonetheless, he found his role as president exhausting and longed to return to the classroom. He submitted his resignation in the spring of 1920. At the request of the Board, he reconsidered and remained at Dakota Wesleyan until his contract expired in 1922. The selection of Edward D. Kohlstedt as the president of Dakota Wesleyan University was made official by the annual meeting of the Board of Directors in June 1922.

Edward Kohlstedt, a graduate of Garrett Biblical Institute, had served the Wisconsin Conference prior to his presidency at Dakota Wesleyan. President Kohlstedt was well-suited to his position; he bonded Conference and community to the college, was a capable fund-raiser, and understood the fundamentals of a first-rate program. The failure of Mitchell's two banks in 1923 due to hard times resulted in a loss of $10,000 in current funds for Dakota Wesleyan. Undaunted, Kohlsted proceeded with a clean-up campaign of $80,000 to wipe out old debts and followed this with a campaign to raise the productive endowment fund to $600,000. This was the amount the North Central Association had set as the minimal sum for a private college with an enrollment of four hundred. At the completion of the campaign, the Board of Directors expressed its gratitude by offering President and Mrs. Kohlstedt a sixty-day vacation for rest and recreation with all expenses paid, and by conferring the honorary degree of Doctor of Law.[10]

Campus improvements included the building of an addition to the east side of Morrow Gymnasium in 1925 to provide dormitory

35

space for college men. Stout Hall, named in honor of Levi Asa Stout, was the last building to be added to the Wesleyan campus until the construction of the new College Hall, an interval of thirty years.

President Kohlstedt also upgraded the quality of instruction at Wesleyan by raising the standard of professional training of the faculty. In 1926 he reported that of a teaching staff of twenty-eight, seven held doctorates and eighteen held master's degrees.[11]

Kohlstedt resigned in 1927 to become executive secretary of the Board of Home Missions and Church Extension. Earl Allen Roadman, a graduate of Boston University School of Theology and member of the Iowa Conference, was chosen as the new executive. Roadman took charge of Dakota Wesleyan on September 1, 1927. Two years and two months later, on Black Friday, the stock market crashed, ushering in the Great Depression. Dakota Wesleyan's long period of progress was halted.

Academic Program

As already indicated, the educational program of Dakota Wesleyan University underwent tremendous change during the years from 1903 to 1930. Changes in course content reflect an ideological shift from revealed truth to rational analysis and pragmatism, as Latin and Greek were replaced by science classes and modern languages. The outward form of a university structure, most closely adhered to during the Nicholson and Kerfoot administrations, was abandoned within a decade as the various "schools" were integrated as departments of the college. There were now three major divisions: the College, the Academy, and the School of Music. The elective system, which reached its apogee in the late nineteenth and early twentieth centuries,[12] was replaced by a group system in 1912, dividing the principal subjects of the collegiate course into four general fields: English, ancient and modern languages, science and mathematics, and history and social studies. Major and minor subjects were introduced as rapidly as course offerings permitted. Each candidate for a degree had to select one major subject for specialization and two minor subjects, chosen from at least two different groups. The aim of this general education program was to insure a broad general knowledge coupled with intensive work in at least two fields. The upgrading of course offerings and the quality of instruction was made possible by the steadily increasing enrollment on the college level.

By 1920 Dakota Wesleyan University had become the largest independent college in the state, with a full-time enrollment of over three hundred. It shared the distinction with the University of South Dakota at Vermillion of being the first in the state to receive accreditation by the North Central Association of Colleges and Secondary Schools.[13] School development reached a plateau in the early 1920s, with enrollment hovering between three hundred and four hundred until the late 1950s.

Growth and change in the collegiate program had been mirrored in the Preparatory Department for many years. It was first officially distinguished from the college in 1904-1905 when Clarence V. Gilliland was named its first principal. In 1907 its name was changed to Academy and a four-year course of study introduced. A four-year high school commercial course was offered in conjunction with the Academy. The two were merged in 1923 and reorganized as a senior high school, offering grades ten to twelve, with tutoring for those lacking ninth grade subjects. The University High School was fully accredited by the State Department of Public Instruction and by the North Central Association of Colleges and Secondary Schools.

Enrollment on the preparatory level dropped decisively in the early twenties as its functions were increasingly taken over by public high schools. This trend was accelerated by the passage of a state law requiring school districts to pay the tuition of students attending public high schools. Cognizant of these facts and faced with the demands of the North Central Association for the separation of college and secondary departments, the Board of Trustees voted to discontinue secondary education at Dakota Wesleyan University with the closing of the spring quarter of 1926. An editorial in the *Phreno Cosmian* voiced the mood of many: "As a University High School, we lower our flag regretfully, but bravely and honorably. This is an age of transition."[14]

Among the areas of vocational training that supplemented the liberal arts program, the School of Education continued to hold first place. It consisted of three separate departments: the Graduate, the Collegiate, and the Normal. The Graduate Department, first advertised in the catalog of 1906, offered both master's and doctor's degrees to those who wished to spend one year or more in advanced study of education. The doctoral program was discontinued in 1908 and the master's in 1913. No doctoral and only one earned master's degree was granted in the history of the school.[15]

37

The Collegiate Department of the School of Education was restricted to college-level work and focused on preparation for high school teaching. The Normal Department gave work on both the high school and college levels and was designed to prepare young men and women to teach in the elementary schools of South Dakota.

The School of Education became the Department of Education in the Liberal Arts College in the reorganization of 1914. All education courses were now on a college level. Graduates of the two-year program were entitled to a state certificate and qualified to teach in the elementary grades. Those preparing for administrative positions and teaching in secondary schools followed a four-year course. The Department of Education grew considerably during the years from 1914 to 1919 and then remained relatively unaltered until 1931.[16]

Second only to the teacher training in the number of students enrolled was the Commercial Department. Commercial courses were offered on both the college and secondary levels and included studies in the general education program. Students completing the four-year college course earned a baccalaureate degree or a Bachelor of Commercial Science degree.

The School of Music came to the forefront during the long teaching tenure of Emery Wilberforce Hobson (1906-1915). Among its eminent teachers was Bernice Frost, a nationally renowned piano pedagogue. The program of the School of Music was designed to meet the needs of three distinct groups: high school students, college students, and those preparing to teach in the field of music. Applied music included instruction in voice, violin, piano and organ. For many years a musical festival was held in May, culminating with an oratorio by the University Choral Union, assisted by guest soloists and orchestras such as the Thomas Orchestra of Chicago and the Minneapolis Symphony Orchestra. Membership in the Choral Union was open to all students and sometimes exceeded one hundred singers. In later years, the mixed singing group was known as the college choir and was accompanied by the college orchestra for its major productions. Of the instrumental groups, the band claims a fairly continuous existence since 1907.

A domestic science laboratory (home economics) installed in the basement of Graham Hall was completed in 1915. A diploma course in nursing in conjunction with the School of Nursing of the new Methodist State Hospital (Mitchell) was first offered in 1918.

38

Of the teachers of this period, none received higher acclaim from their students than the Van Kirks. James was Professor of History from 1920 to 1954. Katherine came to Wesleyan in 1919 and married James two years later. A dearly beloved teacher of English and Latin, her death of cancer in 1930 left the campus in mourning. Other teachers not previously mentioned who were accorded high marks by their students included Dr. Patterson, philosophy; Dr. Hicks, German; Helen Fishbeck, drama and public speaking; and Alvah Beecher, dean of the School of Music.

Student Life and Organizations

Wesleyan students were participants in the real world. In an age of reform, they organized a prohibition league and did their bit to get Mitchell "dry." World War I brought flags, parades, and the pulse of patriotism as troop trains pulled through town. It also brought a poignant sadness. The senior class of 1918, at its last skip day at Firesteel Creek, ate five dozen eggs for breakfast, had military drill, talked about the war, and walked home in the rain.[17] Faculty and students contributed over $1,800 to the YMCA war relief fund in 1917 and sold $10,000 of liberty bonds the following year.

Skirts climbed with the stock market in the Roaring Twenties. Girls at Graham Hall bobbed their hair, dabbled with lipstick, and sneaked an occasional cigarette. The Charleston was secretively danced in society rooms and at the Odd Fellows Lodge downtown. Old timers looked with envy on the modern dormitory facilities, such as steam heat, electric lights, and one telephone for one hundred girls. The two large parlors on the first floor became the new social centers, and ukulele serenades were heard beneath dormitory windows.

Increased enrollment prior to the war brought more mouths than the Graham Hall dining room could conveniently feed. As a consequence, several boarding clubs for young men were organized. A student manager or "buyer" would purchase foods and make all necessary arrangements. Meals were provided at cost. The last boarding club was operated during the peak enrollment following the Armistice. Faced with the soaring cost of food, unpaid accounts, and the resistance of his boarders to meal price hikes, the young entrepreneur J. W. Kaye (later an attorney in Mitchell) bought a carload of potatoes, hawked them by the pound for a good profit, paid his bills, and closed shop.[18]

Numerous social traditions came into being. May Day was observed for many years by the winding of the May pole and an elaborate evening festival staged by the Choral Union at Gale Theater. After a lapse of some years, the Washington Birthday Banquet was again given in 1913 and every year thereafter. The first junior-senior banquet was hosted in a private home in May 1906. Class memorial gifts were begun by the class of 1912. Not content to merely have their names on their diplomas, they inscribed them on a huge granite rock which they moved from the bluffs of the James River to the campus. The class of 1929 used the boulder as a marker when they buried a bottle with class mementos. Fifty years later they were chagrined to learn that the rock had been moved three times during the construction of the new College Hall (now the Matthew D. and Loretta Smith Hall).

One of the major traditions, Blue and White Day, evolved from class scraps that erupted intermittently over the years. One such scrap occurred in the spring of 1910. The freshmen boys, having suffered humiliation at the hands of the sophomore boys, laid careful plans for sweet revenge. In the words of one of the sophomores:

> ...one warm spring evening they fell upon us unawares as we came out one by one from our boarding clubs, quickly tied us up, loaded us into horse drawn taxicabs and drove us into the country. There they gave us partial haircuts with a clipper, branded us with iodine on the forehead with a big "13" and then left us strung along the road, each one tied to a telephone pole.
>
> It didn't take us long to work ourselves free and then we returned to town stopping by St. Joseph's Hospital where a kindly nurse removed the iodine stain from our foreheads. Nothing could be done to hide the clipper haircuts.[19]

It was customary in those days for the seniors to wear their graduation regalia to chapel during their final spring term. The seniors of 1911 were miffed when the juniors removed their robes from the vault and kept them hidden for an entire week before the faculty served notice that they had to be returned. The mode of return was not spelled out, so the juniors hung the robes from hooks in the chapel ceiling under cover of night, but were apprehended by the seniors. Not bothering to get ladders, the seniors smashed holes through the attic ceiling and dropped the robes to the floor. The juniors were severely reprimanded and stuck with a thirty-two dollar bill for repair of the chapel ceiling.[20]

Hoping to defuse such youthful exuberance, President Seaman proclaimed College Day on October 9, 1913. Classes were dismissed for a day of contests and fun, including intramural basketball and football, a bag and a cane rush, a girls' hockey game, and class stunts. The event was billed as Blue and White Day the following year. A push ball contest and a tug of war over a pool of water were added to the activities. The parade and the intercollegiate football game evolved as the main features of the day. A call to college alumni and friends to join the festivities in 1923 initiated Homecoming Day. The original Miss Wesleyan, Carrie Schaeffer, was inaugurated in a simple ceremony on the steps of College Hall in 1929.

Campus social life centered in the literary societies for most of this period. Whereas literary societies throughout the nation were dwindling as many of their features were absorbed into college curricula and the Greek letter fraternity movement became prevalent, they remained active at Dakota Wesleyan but altered their function. Accordingly, when Vice President F.E. Morrison was accosted by a downtown businessman disturbed because a college student had indicated on a job application that she was a member of two "fraternities," Morrison could truthfully assure him that fraternities were banned at Dakota Wesleyan.[21] On campus, however, it was generally recognized that the literary societies had become the functional equivalent of the Greek letter fraternities and sororities. Freshmen were rushed and pledges initiated into society membership with rites of varying secrecy. The "frosh" who received a bid "belonged," whereas the one who failed sometimes felt so crushed that he packed his bags and boarded the next train home. The four society halls (rooms assigned to the societies) were shared by brother and sister teams, and social functions were planned on a brother-sister basis.

Despite strong loyalty to the societies, criticism of them mounted. One student, probably thinking of such closed door activities as dancing and necking, placed the blame for deteriorating standards onto the introduction of mohair davenports and phonographs in the society rooms.[22] The most frequent objections were that the societies militated against school spirit and were undemocratic. One by one, the brother-sister organizations succumbed to the growing popularity of the recreation parlors and the action of the Inter-Society Board barring the pledging of new members. The last feeble remnant of the once powerful societies, the Thalian-Daedalian team, disbanded in 1936.

41

Meanwhile oratory, drama, and debate, the legacy of the literary societies, were gradually absorbed into the English and speech departments. Mastery of the spoken word became the hallmark of this prairie college. In 1924 Wesleyan could boast of twenty-three first place and sixteen second place ratings in the forty-five state oratorical contests that had been held, plus a national championship won by Lloyd Rising in 1918. In addition, Francis Case won top national honors in the 1916 peace oratory contest. Originally open to both men and women, the oratorical contest was later divided into separate competitions referred to as "men's old line" and "women's old line" to differentiate them from other contests. The state association was reorganized as the South Dakota Intercollegiate Forensics Association in 1924.

Debate was started at Dakota Wesleyan around the turn of the century by James Lawrence Lardner. Upon his transferral to Northwestern University, his assistant, Clarion DeWitt Hardy, took charge. In the six intercollegiate state contests between 1914 and 1920, Dakota Wesleyan held five championships and tied for honors in the last. Debate questions were concerned with contemporary and controversial issues such as, "Resolved: that the United States government should own, operate, and control all coal mines within its jurisdiction."[23]

Orators and members of the Dakota Wesleyan varsity teams were selected by a series of inter-society contests. Each society championed its leading speakers and debating teams. University representatives for intercollegiate meets were selected from among these by a faculty committee. General supervision of all forensic activities was assigned to the Dakota Wesleyan Forensic Board, organized in 1916, with three members from the faculty, one member from each of the college literary societies, and one from each of the joint academy societies.

Rivalry in the local eliminations was intense; however, the entire student body rallied with great enthusiasm to support the winners. Special trains carried students to the contests, where they formed a cheering section. Unfortunately, this commendable spirit gradually eroded and gave way to petty divisiveness, leading to the abolishment of all inter-society debates in 1926 by the action of the representatives of the various societies.[24] Forensics came under the official supervision of the speech department. Dakota Wesleyan was granted membership in the Pi Kappa Delta in 1919 in recognition of its achievements in oratory and debate. It was given the state

42

Alpha chapter, being the first college in South Dakota to join this national honorary forensics fraternity.[25]

Student dramatic productions shifted into the regular curriculum well ahead of oratory and debate. Two major productions were scheduled annually. These tended to be either plays of proven merit or contemporary Broadway hits, e.g., "The Rivals" and "Peg O' My Heart." Pageants, recitals, and one-act plays were popular. The operetta "All at Sea" was produced in collaboration with the School of Music in 1926. Major productions were staged at the Metropolitan Theater and later in the junior high school auditorium and the Corn Palace.

A variety of student publications appeared during this period. The *Phreno Cosmian*, following a trend toward a newspaper format, placed increasing emphasis on news coverage. The 1928-1929 issues, edited by C. Maurice Wieting, received top ratings as a college weekly in both state and national press competitions. The need for student literary expression was met by the *Blue and White Book*, produced from 1914 to 1924 by the English Club under the direction of Clyde Tull, professor of English language and literature.

Campus religious organizations continued to show exceptional vitality. These included the Life and Service Club, the Oxford Club for ministerial students, a large Student Volunteer Band, and the giant of them all, the "Y"s (Young Men's Christian Association and Young Women's Christian Association). If there was a job that needed doing, the "Y"s did it. A bewildered young man arriving for his first day of college was met at the depot by "Y" fellows who showed him where to go, how to register, and what books to buy. Needy students were assisted in finding jobs. A stag reception was given to chase the blues, followed by an all-school reception some days later. One lonely freshman girl wrote home:

> The Y.W.C.A. seems the warmest spot here. One afternoon they served tea and it was lovely meeting all the new girls. That evening ten of us were taken to a beautiful home in town and we had pears and music. In twenty minutes we went to another house and had candy and games, then in a third home we had popcorn and practiced remembering each other's names. When we started back a mob of little boys followed us, took hold of our arms, hugged us and did comical things. We asked who they were and the little scamps said they were the Y.M.C.A.[26]

The YMCA also continued to sponsor the annual lecture series, later known as the Lyceum course. Patrons exchanged standing room at the Court House for the cushioned seats of the Gale Theater until it was destroyed by fire in 1914. Subsequent lecturers appeared at the Methodist Church. Proceeds from the lectures were used to buy needed equipment.

Prior to the hiring in 1926 of C. K. Mahoney as director of campus religious activities, the "Y"s coordinated the religious life of the school except for chapel and the annual evangelistic meetings. Sunday afternoon YMCA services drew overflow attendance and had to be moved to the Methodist Church. The YWCA held a similar meeting in Graham Hall at the same hour. Midweek prayer meetings had good student participation, including football players who came for a half hour of meditation before going to the practice field. In later years, Sunday afternoon student forums were held at Prexy Lodge. These centered around such titles as E. Stanley Jones' *Christ of the Indian Road* and Kirtley F. Mather's *Science in Search of God*, reflecting the religious concerns of the Scopes monkey trial decade.

Wesleyan's motto, "Sacrifice or Service," found full expression in the Student Volunteer Band, an affiliate of the "Y"s. Its membership consisted of students who were planning for Christian service vocations. Gospel teams were active in the churches of the area and undertook such projects as supervising summer baseball for young boys. A large number of the Student Volunteers entered foreign missions, especially to Latin America, China, and India. Interest in India missions was fostered by the Schermerhorns, who had served there. Dakota Wesleyan's impact for good in this area is exemplified by the work of the Carhart family — Raymond and Edith (Mexico), Walter and Ethel (Chili), Florence (Chili); Amber Van (Japan); by medical missionaries such as Frank and Bessie Beck (Bolivia) and Reno Backus (China); and by educators such as Matthew D. and Loretta Smith (Mexico, Peru, and Panama); Leona Burr (China and Japan); and Kenneth M. and Marguerite Harkness (missionaries to Mozambique, Africa and educators in Japan, Korea and Nepal). In order to perpetuate their interest in Christian higher education at Dakota Wesleyan, Kenneth, Marguerite, and their three sons funded a $150,000 Harkness Memorial Fund.

Organized sports occupied a growing place in campus life. Shortly after the turn of the century, the colleges of the area joined colleges of North Dakota and Minnesota to form the Minnesota-Dakota Conference. It was short-lived because of travel distance and lack of gate receipts. Representatives of the old competitors, Huron College, Sioux Falls College, Yankton College, and Dakota Wesleyan, met in March 1917 to discuss their mutual athletic problems. "This led to the organization of the South Dakota Intercollegiate Athletic Conference at Mitchell on September 24, 1917, with the above schools and the School of Mines (Rapid City) and Northern Normal (Aberdeen) as charter members. The number was brought to ten with the admission of Augustana College (Sioux Falls), Eastern Normal (Madison), Southern Normal (Springfield), and Spearfish Normal. Columbus College (Chamberlain) and Redfield College (Redfield) were members for a brief time only. Annual competitive events were scheduled between member schools in football, basketball, and track until 1940, when the SDIAC was reorganized."[27]

Football was a favorite sport. Athletes scrimmaged on the gridiron while the legislators in Pierre debated bills to ban the game. On Thanksgiving Day morning in 1925, over three hundred boosters for Wesleyan's Tigers, including practically the entire student body and faculty, boarded six coaches chartered as a special non-stop train to see the tussle between the Tigers and the Greyhounds at Yankton that forenoon. The special half-rate fare for the round trip was $2.70.[28] The Tigers were whipped in that game; nonetheless, they made a creditable record in intercollegiate football competitions and were frequent conference champions. Mark Payne set a world record with a drop kick of sixty-three yards in a game with Aberdeen in 1915. Richard "Bud" Dougherty coached all sports at Dakota Wesleyan in the eight years following World War I, during which time Wesleyan had more than its share of victories and conference championships.

Interest in basketball developed slowly at Dakota Wesleyan. The players practiced at City Hall and engaged in intramural contests and skirmishes with businessmen's teams. Provision of a practice floor in Morrow Gymnasium and the inclusion of basketball as a competitive sport in the SDIAC quickly raised it to first place among winter sports.

Recreational activity shifted to the baseball diamond and the tennis courts with the coming of spring. Tennis enjoyed great popularity. An annual local tournament was sponsored by the Tennis Association to select representatives in the state tournament. Opportunity for swimming was provided by the new pool in Morrow Gymnasium, and an annual spring water carnival was presented by

45

the Dolphin Club. Except for football, girls generally engaged in the same sports as boys. These included volleyball, archery, hiking, and hockey in addition to those already mentioned. Policies pertaining to athletics were in the hands of the Athletic Board, a joint committee of students and faculty formed in 1916. The Mitchell Athletic Association, largely downtown businessmen, raised money for needed facilities. Men who had been awarded monograms for participation in athletic events were eligible for membership in the "W" Club.

Student government at Dakota Wesleyan was vested in the Student Association, of which every student was a member, and the Inter-Society Council. The real clout in campus politics was wielded by the literary societies. Nominations were fought out on a society basis and elections were permeated with inter-society spirit. Independents could swing an election only if the fight was close. The power of the societies was curtailed by the new Student Association Constitution adopted in 1916. The Student Senate now became the primary governing body and controlled student activity through four boards: the Athletic Board, the Forensic Board, the Inter-Society Board and the Phreno Cosmian Board. The same year brought a measure of self-government to the women in the college dormitories with the organization of the Women's House Government Association. The name was changed to Women's Self-Government Association in 1920.

The Alumnal Association of Dakota Wesleyan University was formed in 1922 with Francis Case as president. It replaced the former Alumni Association. All former students and graduates were eligible for membership. The first Alumni bulletin was printed for the first Homecoming Day in 1923. Alumnal clubs were organized in numerous cities, serving as a continuing contact between the college and former students.

Financial Overview and Summary

Monetary support remained a basic problem for Dakota Wesleyan. The college's fiscal problems had a hard core. Located in an area of marginal economy and sparse population, Dakota Wesleyan University competed for the students and dollars available with numerous other state and denominational schools. The financial resources of its supporting constituency were limited and largely dependent upon agriculture. The school's investments were also chiefly in lands. Consequently, it was impossible to liquidate indebtedness and build a satisfactory endowment fund despite efficient business management. John Prince Jenkins, for many years field agent for Dakota Wesleyan, described his efforts as follows:

> The year now closing (1911-1912) has demanded of one trying to raise money, a severe test of faith and perseverence...The hot winds came and stayed with us, until small grain prospects were entirely blasted, and the progress of my canvass was checked at once, and cannot be recovered until another harvest is well assured.

> I have worked during this past winter in localities where the people were to be dependent upon their county to furnish them grain for this spring's sowing...Money has been almost impossible to get. The people have become exceedingly cautious and in many cases very apprehensive. The farmers are universally hard up.[29]

Church support for Dakota Wesleyan came from three sources: the Dakota Conference, the Methodist Board of Home Missions, and the Methodist Board of Education. Substantial support from the Dakota Conference was given in 1925-1926 when President Kohlstedt launched a drive for endowment to retain North Central accreditation. The goal of $600,000 was reached and accreditation retained.

Student tuition rates rose from fifty dollars to one hundred seventy dollars between 1910 and 1930. The rise was not nearly so steep if adjusted for inflation. Approximately two-thirds of the students received financial support from the school in the form of employment, college loan funds, Methodist loan funds, or rebated fees.

A consideration of the financial aspects of Dakota Wesleyan University during these years would not be complete without mention of John F. Way, secretary-treasurer of the college and manager of the business offices for twenty years (1910-1930). "Uncle John" conducted the business details of the college with great efficiency until advanced age prompted him to retire. The resignation of his son, Walter, who had been manager of the University bookstore and assistant to his father, was accepted at the same time.

In summary, Dakota Wesleyan University grew from a "prep" school with a fragmentary college program in 1903 to a fully developed four-year college by 1920. The growing emphasis on the collegiate department and the broader educational background of the enrollees made a more sophisticated program possible. The quality of instruction underwent tremendous upgrading as teachers were required to have professional training in the fields they taught and earned degrees became commonplace and even mandatory. The boast that Dakota Wesleyan University was South Dakota's biggest and best accredited independent college was not without foundation. It was a formative force in the church, the community, and throughout the world. The statement of John Prince Jenkins to the Board of Directors in 1914 was still apropos in 1930:

> We have much to acquire...but considering our age and the newness of the state, I believe we have planned, wrought, and achieved well. I have written this in order that we might "thank God and take courage."[30]

Courage was indeed needed to face the days ahead.

Chapter IV

Built on a Rock:
1930-1952

Administrative Highlights

It fell to President Earl A. Roadman to guide Dakota Wesleyan University through the dirtiest of the 1930s. The economic paralysis that gripped the nation in the wake of the financial collapse of 1929 was compounded throughout the Great Plains by a severe and prolonged drought. Dust storms brought darkness at noonday and hordes of grasshoppers devoured meager crops. Outmigration reduced the state's population from 692,849 in 1930 to 642,961 in 1940.

Wesleyan's income was severely curtailed by the inability of students to pay tuition costs, the termination of support by the Methodist Board of Education, and the loss of nearly all income from endowment investments. By the spring of 1932 it became obvious that drastic steps had to be taken if the college doors were to remain open. President Roadman's recollection of these years was as follows:

> It was desperate; it was terrible. On one occasion the Board of Dakota Wesleyan spent an entire session deciding whether or not to change the boilers of our furnace to burn corn instead of coal. At ten cents a bushel, we could have bought corn and burned it at half the price of coal. But there was an objection to burning food. We accepted wheat at seventy-five cents per bushel when the farmer could have gotten only twenty-five. We accepted corn, we accepted chickens, we accepted pork, we accepted everything that would make it possible for students to come to school.[1]

The budget for 1932-1933 was slashed by nearly one-third. Faculty and staff were reduced, library allotments cut, plans for improvement cancelled, and all but the most necessary repairs postponed.

49

Every effort was made not to reduce curricular offerings.[2] This resulted in heavier teaching loads and increased auxiliary responsibilities. When Melvin W. Hyde, dean of the college, was questioned, "Just what does a dean do?" by a member of the Board, he replied:

> In addition to the administrative duties of the Dean's office, it has been my privilege to carry two-thirds of a teaching load. Additional work during the year which has been mine includes the directing of the publicity activities for the college, the publicity for the Fiftieth Anniversary Campaign, supervision of the Registrar's office during the first half of the year, director of the Placement Bureau, faculty athletic representative, teacher of the freshman Sunday School class, president of the Men's Brotherhood, besides numerous committee responsibilities in college, church, and state educational associations.[3]

Scarcity of cash made it impossible to pay even meager salaries. During the height of the Depression only 60 percent of faculty salary was guaranteed. Of the remainder, up to 25 percent was paid in non-cash items such as board at Graham Hall, tuition and music lessons for faculty families, county and district school warrants, and merchandise coupons at Mitchell stores. A portion of this salary was commonly returned to the University for such purposes as assisting needy students and special campaigns, such as the thirty-dollars-a-day drive, which sought a donor for that amount for each day of the year.

To make it possible for students to continue their education, room and board rates were reduced and financial assistance was provided in the form of job opportunities, student loans, and federal assistance through the National Youth Administration (NYA) program. Accepting an indigent student body resulted in a fairly stable enrollment but did little for the treasury. Nonetheless, it was a commendable policy in that it enabled youth to utilize their growing years creatively in an era when unemployment and despondency were widespread, thereby enriching both themselves and society.

Being the business manager of a private, plains state college during the Depression era was a formidable task, but Harmon Brown ('22) coped. Reared in South Dakota, Brown had graduated from Wesleyan "on half a shoe string" and was renowned for his ability to dicker and deal. On one occasion he called President Roadman to accompany him and a doctor to a farm. Roadman relates:

...A farmer had offered to trade three cows, which hadn't seen a blade of grass for days, if the doctor would take them from him at seventy-five dollars a head upon a long overdue account. The doctor proposed to Harmon that he would accept the farmer's suggestion if Harmon would take the cows at fifty dollars per head upon his son's tuition at the college. The deal was clinched right there.

When we got home I offered Harmon sixty dollars for the least desirable looking cow in the trio. I never will forget her slit ear and beseeching look. But I was thinking of our kids and the udder side of the cow looked promising...[4]

By such innovative strategies and the unfailing support of members of the Board, faculty, townsmen, and parishioners of the Dakota Conference, themselves hard pressed, was the margin of survival provided.

Conditions had improved slightly by the school's fiftieth anniversary in 1935, and full-time enrollment had reached an all-time high. The Golden Jubilee campaign netted $100,000. It was used for endowment, improvement of buildings, and reduction of indebtedness. "Fifty Golden Years," a pageant by Mrs. H. C. Culver representing Wesleyan's history, was presented by a cast of five hundred persons at the Corn Palace in Mitchell on June 1, 1935. Over nineteen thousand students had enrolled at Wesleyan during its first half century, and its alumni encircled the globe.

Roadman was an astute administrator and had exceptional rapport with the younger generation. However, his attempt to liberalize the school's position on dancing put him on a collision course with conservative pastors of the Dakota Conference. Supervised dancing at Dakota Wesleyan was approved by the Board of Directors at a November 1933 meeting. Subsequently, all-college dances were scheduled monthly at Morrow Gymnasium with parties for non-dancers held simultaneously at Graham Hall. A questionnaire revealed little opposition among faculty and parents, and many students danced in their home communities. Nonetheless, objection from Conference pastors was so strong that it became a factor in Roadman's resignation, assured the election of Leon Sweetland as president in the spring of 1936, and led to the suspension of dancing under University auspices shortly afterwards.

President Roadman resigned in mid-April 1936 to accept the presidency of Morningside College of Sioux City, Iowa, a post he held for twenty years. He returned for commencement exercises in June to present the diplomas to the graduating class, which included two of his children. Meanwhile, Leon Sweetland served as acting president.

Sweetland, a graduate of Garrett Biblical Institute and Northwestern University, had been president of Montana Wesleyan College at Helena from 1917 to 1919 and served pastorates in various states. His election as president of Dakota Wesleyan University was made official on June 10, 1936.[5]

President Sweetland gave strong support to the conservatives in the Dakota Conference on their opposition to dancing and their "supreme right" to set standards for campus social life. He curtailed student government and imposed strict rules of conduct.[6] The students were in no mood to comply with authoritarian decrees and became openly defiant by spring.[7]

The foment spread from the University community to the business sector of town and the outposts of the Dakota Conference. A student petition requesting policy changes was presented to the Board on February 16, 1937, and a special committee was appointed to investigate allegations against the President.[8] The Board of Directors convened in a special meeting on May 22, 1937. The investigating committee made its report in an executive session after which all materials were destroyed. The meeting reconvened in open session, at which Sweetland was exonerated of all moral charges. The break, however, had become too serious to bridge. Sweetland was advised to use his prerogative as a Methodist minister to secure another appointment. His resignation was accepted at the same session.[9]

Ira G. McCormack was chosen to succeed Sweetland, but declined the position, whereupon Joseph H. Edge was elected on July 3, 1937. Joseph Henry Edge graduated from Boston University and united with the Northwest Iowa Conference prior to assuming the presidency of Dakota Wesleyan University.

Dakota had experienced seven consecutive crop failures when "Joe" Edge took office. One of his first actions was the establishment of a revolving student loan fund of $75,000 to assist indigent students. Improvement in the economy and funds allotted to the University by the Methodist Crusade for Christ[10] made possible the most urgent repairs on buildings and equipment. Campus changes during Edge's incumbency included the remodeling of Prexy Lodge and its assignment to the School of Music. A formal opening was held on December 1, 1937. The John F. Way home at 1120 East University was renovated and used as the president's residence. A newly lighted football field and a steel stadium were completed in time for the clash between the Tigers and the Vikings on Blue and White Day in 1941.

A new cultural organization, the Friends of the Middle Border, an affiliate of Dakota Wesleyan, was formed in 1939. Its purpose was to preserve and foster an appreciation for the regional culture of the upper Missouri River valley, an area designated as the Middle Border by Hamlin Garland, Dakota author and incorporating member of the FMB. The principal founder, charter member and main force of the museum and the art gallery was Leland D. Case (ex'22), a well-known editor and journalist. He later endowed the corporation. FMB materials were displayed at College Hall until 1954, when a building was erected one block east of Graham Hall with funds left to the FMB by Grace B. Jordan. It housed a social history museum, the Dakota galleries, a territorial textbook collection, and the Jennewein Western American Library, a gift of J. Leonard Jennewein and the class of 1912. The presence of the FMB fostered interest in regional history and literature at Dakota Wesleyan University.

The decade of the thirties had opened with severe drought and a national economic collapse. It ended with Adolph Hitler's rise to power and the outbreak of World War II in Europe on September 3, 1939. The United States entered the war following the bombing of Pearl Harbor by the Japanese on December 7, 1941. Courses in officer training were made available at Dakota Wesleyan University through cooperation with federal programs. A large percentage of the male students were in the enlisted Reserves. As a result, curricular emphasis shifted to physics, mathematics, and physical education.[11] A total of 232 Wesleyan students had joined the military forces by the fall of 1942. Enrollment dropped to 130 in the fall of 1944, severely impacting education programs and the budget. Student labor problems were reversed, with the college forced to hire outsiders to fill student positions. A number of students of Oriental ancestry were enrolled through the Japanese-American Relocation Committee.

Dakota Wesleyan lost the appearance of a women's college with the coming of V-J Day in 1945. Veterans returned to continue their education under the G. I. Bill of Rights, and revisions in the selective service procedure permitted high school seniors to enroll in college courses. This influx began during the last year of President

Edge's administration. He tendered his resignation, effective September 1, 1946, on the twenty-sixth of May.

Two men received favorable consideration for the office of president in the fall of 1946. Samuel Hilburn, who had been selected as the alternate, assumed the duties of chief executive at Dakota Wesleyan on the first of November, when Robert Burns accepted the presidency of the College of the Pacific. Following overseas duty during World War I, Samuel Milton Hilburn matriculated at Southern Methodist University and spent two terms as a missionary to Japan under the sponsorship of the Methodist Episcopal Church South. He earned a doctorate from the University of Chicago while on furlough. Compelled to leave the Orient at the outbreak of the war, the family returned to the United States. Hilburn was an instructor in a naval intelligence school at Boulder, Colorado at the time of his call to Mitchell.

There were many new faces on the Wesleyan campus in the fall of 1946. Enrollment had nearly quadrupled, with the freshman class constituting over one-half of the student body. Nearly the same proportion were G.I.s receiving their education under the G. I. Bill of Rights. Men outnumbered women two to one. Married veterans, a new phenomenon on college campuses, were housed in government surplus trailer units grouped just south of Science Hall and in the area where the north wing of Dayton Hall is now located. New faculty and administrative appointments numbered twenty-two out of forty-two, including the dean of the college, the dean of women, the business manager, and the president.[12]

There was also a new educational program. A planning committee had been set up by the Board of Directors for the purpose of formulating a new educational approach. President Hilburn, who was hired to inaugurate and direct this program, had some well-defined ideas of his own which he promoted vigorously. Centered on the concept of "integrated education," the new program emphasized human relations, the integration of courses, and the individualized approach, the process of education being conceived of in terms of personal development rather than specified coursework.[13]

The new plan was fully operative by the 1948-1949 school term and received favorable national recognition, but lacked support locally. Opposition from members of the faculty and Board surfaced almost immediately. Conference endorsement was not forthcoming. Hilburn's de-emphasis of athletics engendered disfavor, and his expressed opinion of America's shared responsibility for the war with Japan was unpopular with veteran students and gave rise to downtown rumors of un-American ideologies on the "hill."

Far more devastating was the sharp drop in enrollment and the impending financial crisis. College enrollments throughout the nation had crested between 1946 and 1948 as returning veterans entered school. The decline in numbers in the years following was significantly sharper at Dakota Wesleyan than at other area colleges, as student transfers increased. By 1950 the accumulated deficit had ballooned from $43,000 to $132,793 and had become a millstone around the neck of the new program. Accrediting agencies became concerned. The full-time faculty was reduced by a third for the school year of 1951-1952. Hilburn's resignation was accepted at the annual meeting of the Board in May 1951.[14] An administrative committee consisting of Jesse Knox, dean; Wendell Walton, public relations; and Gordon Rollins, business manager, was appointed to handle the affairs of the school. Matthew D. Smith, an alumnus and former dean of Dakota Wesleyan University, was elected president on November 14, 1951.

Academic Program

Turning to a consideration of curricular organization, we note that the group system adopted in Seaman's administration was replaced by a divisional plan in 1938. Courses were divided into five areas: natural sciences and mathematics, social sciences, philosophy and religion, languages and literature, and the fine arts. Both divisional and departmental majors were offered. General education requirements totaled over sixty quarter hours plus physical education.

Dakota Wesleyan tended to follow the conventional curricular patterns of the liberal arts colleges. A period of limited innovation and conscious attempt to style the educational program at Wesleyan in accordance with its distinctive Christian aims and cultural setting became apparent in the thirties and culminated during Hilburn's administration.[15] This experimental educational program, previously discussed, was cut short by monetary imperatives before its educational value could be ascertained.

Teacher training, under the able direction of Melvin Hyde, remained one of Wesleyan's major functions. The backbone of the program continued to be a four-year course leading to certification for entering secondary education and a two-year course designed for those who wished to enter elementary education.

A significant shift from elementary to secondary education training and from rural to city placement occurred during these years as rural students boarded the big yellow bus to attend consolidated schools in nearby towns and a high school education became the norm. Over 50 percent of the graduates between the years of 1936 and World War II went into rural teaching, contrasted with a scant 6 percent in the decade following the war.[16] A campus professional teachers' organization, the Levi Asa Stout Chapter of the Future Teachers of America, was formed in 1944.[17]

The department of home economics offered a four-year course from 1931 to 1947 which met the requirements for the high school general certificate for teaching home economics under the Smith-Hughes plan.

The School of Music rose to prominence under the tutelage of Alvah Beecher (1929-1934). Degree courses included a B.A. or B.S. with a music major or minor; a Bachelor of Music course for those with professional career interests; and a Bachelor of Music Education for music teachers. The newly formed A Cappella Choir and the Glee Clubs toured the state and large cities. Beecher also organized and directed the Mitchell Philharmonic Society. He was succeeded by Thomas Williams. These were the School of Music's finest hours. Enrollment reached a peak of 292 in 1931-1932, declined as the recession wore on, and did not recoup its numbers.

The music and drama departments collaborated in staging operettas and original productions, such as the folk opera, "He's Gone Away," given in conjunction with the Middle Border Days in 1951. Drama groups such as the Prairie Players were closely aligned with church activities.

The groundwork for the dramatic arts was laid by Helen Fishbeck Holgate (1926-1933). By the early thirties they were firmly established in the program of the University. A period of slow but steady development followed. The accumulation of production materials and the construction of a chapel stage in 1938 facilitated dramatic renditions. The drama community was widened to include neighboring schools and the city. There were workshops for high schools, a children's theater, and support for a community theater.[18] Opportunity for radio drama was provided by a time allotment on KORN, the Mitchell broadcasting station, beginning in 1936. A two-year course in newspaper journalism was set up with the advice and aid of W. R. Ronald, editor of the *Mitchell Daily Republic.*

Oscar Howe, state artist laureate, was named artist-in-residence in 1948 and served on the art faculty. Howe, a Yankton Sioux from the Crow Creek Indian Reservation, earned his BA degree from Wesleyan in 1952. Howe sold some of his paintings to meet college costs. "He came to the door with a painting," Loretta Smith recalled. "I agreed to buy it and asked what he wanted. When he said 'Twenty-five dollars,' I was a bit taken aback. That was a lot of money in those days, but we got it together."[19] Howe designed the murals for the Corn Palace for many years and gained international fame as a portrayer of Sioux Indian life.

Teachers of merit to be added to those already mentioned include Ken Otis, biology; Ralph Dunbar, chemistry; Chester Rich, commerce; and George McGovern, history and forensics.

A resurgence of interest in forensics drew Dakota Wesleyan into numerous competitions and tournaments. George McGovern and Matthew Smith, Jr. set an outstanding record in the Red River Valley Forensic Tournament of 1943 by taking first place in men's debate and also ranking first and second, respectively, as the highest-ranking speakers at the meet. Wesleyan claimed twenty championships in main field oratory in the sixty-four contests held between 1888 and 1942. Donna Comstock became the third to gain the national crown by placing first in women's old line in 1948.[20]

Student Life and Organizations

One of the factors shaping student life was the ever-increasing number of cars on campus. Ernest A. Carhart recalled:

> ...coming to the campus from St. Morgan, Colo. with my sister Maurine and my cousin Melvin Bauman in his little red Ford coupe. Mel and I had shaved, using hot water out of the radiator and the car mirror. We drove around the campus and about the first person we met was Prexy Roadman. We were amazed that the president of the college should take the time to guide us around and give us a tour of the university. Prexy was like that...(Incidentally, we found Mel's car in the hole they dug and filled with water for the yearly tug of war on Blue and White Day one morning.)[21]

Mel ('33) later returned to Wesleyan and served as director of public relations and admissions and alumni activities for fourteen years.

Alumni of the thirties reported that lack of cash often kept the gas tank empty and put a crimp on social activities. Most students worked to meet college costs, leaving little time for fun. They walked to the Corn Palace for basketball games, where LaVerne "Hub" Hubbard pepped them up with his energetic cheerleading. They walked downtown to dance at Dreamland and, like Cinderella, sometimes stayed too long, only to find their speedy return to Graham Hall blocked by freight trains (there was no overpass). One coed reported frequent confinement to the dorm as penalty for coming in after set hours.[22] Dancing returned to the campus in 1950.

The "Rec" in the basement of College Hall was a popular hangout for gab fests, listening to the radio, checkers, chess, and ping-pong tournaments. Members of the literary societies socialized in the two halls shared by brother and sister societies until 1936 when they disbanded.

One of the worst pranks ever perpetrated at Dakota Wesleyan involved a cow that joined a college fraternity. The cow was put in one of the society rooms on the third floor of College Hall on a Friday night and was not discovered until Monday morning.

> It would have been a strain upon the language of the gutter if one had sought to describe the davenports, love seats, the curtains and the carpet in that hall. Who did it? Of course it was done by members of the rival fraternity.[23]

Hoping to blunt the threat of a massive retaliation, the administration made full restoration to the aggrieved societies for the purchase of new furnishings. The ringleader of the plot was never apprehended.

Among the traditions retained at Dakota Wesleyan was initiation, with its freshman beanies and kangaroo court. Frosh carried long memories of such hazing as cracking a raw egg in the mouth and swallowing it and trips around the track in gym while upperclassmen used wooden paddles. Other traditions included the Washington Birthday Banquet, the junior-senior banquet and prom, and Blue and White Day. A bonfire and snake dance were added to the latter in 1937. The annual stunt night gave way to a banquet for students and alumni a few years later. Inaugural ceremonies for Miss Wesleyan were moved to the college chapel in 1940, with the University president participating. Jerry Parkinson and Roberta McRae, elected by popular vote as the first king and queen to reign over homecoming, were crowned in 1950. The selection of Miss

Wesleyan and the Scotchman, based on character, scholarship and overall contribution to the University, was moved to spring. Homecoming Day became an opportune time for official school ceremonies and special anniversary observances.

Wesleyan's "original" panty raid was staged by the few men remaining on campus during war years. Having locked Katherine Druse, dean of women, securely in her room at Graham Hall, the invaders threw the master switch, plunging the dormitory into darkness. Beds were overturned, drawers emptied, and closets ransacked. As the cry, "Everybody out!" rang through the halls, the intruders vanished.[24]

The *Phreno Cosmian* continued as the official school publication. Ethel Johnson Hughes shared her experience as editor in 1945:

> At that time it was the policy that the paper be self-supporting. An editor and business manager were elected by the student body, and they were responsible for the success of the paper. If they ended up in the red, they had to pay the debt personally. Wayne Williamson was business manager the year I was the editor, and I'm happy to say that we paid our bills and had a little money left over, which we got to keep. The paper was printed downtown at the Mitchell *Gazette* office. The linotype operator was usually drunk, but very good to us, and the boss was very sober and strict. So we dealt with both as best we could.[25]

The *Tumbleweed* was published annually after 1948. A new magazine, the *Prairie Wind*, authored by the Writers' Club, replaced the *Blue and White Book*.

Campus religious organizations underwent considerable flux during these years. "Y" gospel teams continued the work of the Student Volunteer Band that had faded out in the late twenties. However, interest in the "Y"s was waning. The men's and women's associations merged in 1943 and were soon discontinued. Their role as coordinator of campus religious activities was taken over by the director of religious activities and the Religious Life Council, composed of faculty and students. Their main concerns were the assembly and chapel services and the annual religious emphasis week. The Kappa Chi and the Methodist Student Movement emerged as the leading campus religious organizations.

A chapter of the Kappa Chi was formed at Wesleyan in 1941. Its membership ranged from thirty to fifty students who were preparing for church-related vocations. Its projects included the publication of a Lenten devotional booklet and deputation teams which provided leadership for Sunday morning worship services, rallies, and the like. The Methodist Student Movement, a nationwide branch of the Methodist Church for the promotion of campus ministries, was organized locally in 1948. The MSM sponsored Friday morning devotionals in the Upper Room in College Hall, a Sunday morning study group at the First Methodist Church, Saturday afternoon hymn sings at the Methodist Hospital, and parties for the children at Abbott House, a children's home adjacent to the campus.

Collegiate sports played an ever-growing role in higher education throughout the nation and at Wesleyan. Nothing surpassed a winning football team for a show of school spirit. Administrators saw good athletic programs as an asset in recruiting students and in enhancing the school treasury. South Dakota's state and church colleges had been members of the South Dakota Intercollegiate Athletic Conference since 1917. In 1940 they split into two groups. The denominational colleges (Huron, Dakota Wesleyan, Augustana, Yankton, and Sioux Falls) withdrew to form the South Dakota College Conference. The state-controlled schools (Eastern, Mines, Northern, Southern, and Spearfish) retained the name of the original organization. The reason for the withdrawal was economic; games with state schools involved more travel expenses and netted less in gate receipts. Wesleyan also joined the Dakota-Iowa Conference in the forties, thus participating in two Conferences, but dropped its membership in the DIC in 1949. The publics and privates, with the exception of Augustana College, reorganized in 1948-49 to form the South Dakota Intercollegiate Conference, thereby renewing a long-standing association.[26]

Stuart Ferguson, alumnus and football coach from 1929 to 1934, set Wesleyan's top win-lose record of 71-17, or 80 percent. Ferguson led the Tigers to four Conference championships and three Amateur Athletic Union tournaments. The only undefeated regular (non-Conference) football season in Wesleyan's history was 1931-1932 with a 17-0 win-lose ratio. There was no football at Dakota Wesleyan during the war years of 1943 to 1945, but the Tigers rebounded 4-0 in 1945-46 and were crowned state champions.[27]

Records in interscholastic competitions show that the Wesleyan Tigers slipped somewhat in football, improved in track, and soared to the top in basketball. The Blue and White cagers participated in eight national basketball tournaments between 1937 and 1947, winning more games in the NAIA competitions than any other

60

school in the Dakotas.[28] Lester Belding, director of athletics from 1935 to 1943 and 1944 to 1945, also built up an outstanding intramural program with a wide range of activities designed to involve all students.

Summary

Economic crises were normative for Dakota Wesleyan University during the years 1930 to 1952. Depression, out-migration, loss of endowment income, wars, and administrative debacles came in rapid succession or concurrently. It is significant that no new buildings or major improvements were added to the campus during this period. It is surprising, therefore, that full-time student enrollment remained fairly constant, fluctuating between three and four hundred, with a low of 144 in 1944-1945 and a high of 445 in 1947-1948. Both figures are directly related to World War II. Despite the strictures of the times, Dakota Wesleyan continued to carry out its mission.

Chapter V

Out of Disaster Into a New Day: 1952-1969

Administrative Highlights

Matthew Dinsdale Smith took office as President of Dakota Wesleyan University on March 1, 1952, the first alumnus and the first lay person to hold that position. Born in Wisconsin, Smith grew to manhood at Alpena, South Dakota. He graduated from Dakota Wesleyan in 1912, attended Columbia University and received a doctorate in education from the University of California in 1930. His life career in education was divided between Methodist colleges in the States and educational ventures in Latin America under the aegis of the Board of Missions of the Methodist church. While teaching at the Anglo-American School at Calloa, Peru (1917-1920) he met and wed Loretta Sage, his lifelong companion and co-worker. Smith was president of the Mexican Methodist Institute of Puebla, Mexico from 1922 to 1932; dean of Kansas Wesleyan University from 1932 to 1936; dean of Dakota Wesleyan University from 1936 to 1944; and director of the Pan-American Institute, Panama City, Panama from 1944 to 1952.

Rumors of the closing of the college abounded when Smith took office. Quiet and unobtrusive, he set about to restore confidence in the school. His ability to gain personal loyalty and build grass roots support stood him in good stead. "The task that confronted me was a discouraging one which I might not have assumed if I had been able to see the whole picture," wrote Smith, "but love for Alma Mater was strong and I had faith in the future of the institution."[1] A twenty-year loan of $125,000 at 4 percent interest was received from Midland Life Insurance Company, Watertown, upon the recommendation of its secretary, John Ehrstrom, an alumnus and trustee of Wesleyan. This bolstered Wesleyan's credit and helped to start it on the road to economic recovery.[2] Long-term goals projected for the commemoration of Dakota Wesleyan's seventy-fifth anniversary in 1960 were five-fold: an enrollment of five hundred; a 20 percent increase in faculty salaries; a new women's dormitory; renovation of College Hall; and a productive endowment of one million dollars.[3] The South Dakota Foundation of Private Colleges was organized during the first summer of the Smith administration, with Augustana, Huron, Sioux Falls, Yankton, and Dakota Wesleyan as founding members. This cooperative approach has benefited member schools in the procurement of financial gifts from businesses and large corporations.

Of special benefit to University personnel and their families was the adoption of Social Security and supplemental programs. Dr. Charles L. Calkins ('17), executive secretary of the Board of Pensions of The Methodist Church, Evanston, and a member of the DWU Board of Trustees, methodically encouraged the trustees and college to adopt Social Security, plus a joint group hospital-medical program and a retirement program to augment Social Security. In 1952 the trustees, faculty and staff voted to enter the Social Security program. Shortly thereafter a group health insurance program was adopted. In 1958 the trustees, faculty and staff approved the entrance into a retirement program with Teachers Insurance Annuity Association-College Retirement Equities Fund (TIAA-CREF), whereby the enrolled employee would contribute 5 percent of salary and this amount would be matched by the college.[4]

Wesleyan was steadily moving toward recovery when disaster struck on February 12, 1955. College Hall, the oldest building on campus and center of academic activities for sixty-six years, was gutted by a flash blaze. The fire was reported at 12:50 on Saturday afternoon. Within two and one-half hours the interior had burned out, the bell tower fallen, and part of two walls crumbled. The remaining outer walls stood as charred sentinels over the glowing embers. Fallen stone and debris broke the central heating pipes in the tunnel beneath the building. This break shut off the steam providing heat for Graham Hall where women students lived and all students ate. That same afternoon, in spite of two-below-zero weather, Swanson Plumbing and Heating Company was on hand with steam pipes and baled straw to lay a temporary steam line above ground, covered with straw bales, to provide heat to Graham Hall before nightfall.[5]

Consumed by the flames was a library of thirty thousand books, classrooms and administrative offices, the student recreational center, and all radio equipment for college station KDWU, operative since 1952. Loss in cash value to the Friends of the Middle Border stood at about fifty thousand dollars, many items being irreplaceable. These included valuable books, maps and taped recordings, the Thomas Morrell collection, original manuscripts of Badger Clark, and other items. Many of these materials had been kept at College Hall to prevent deterioration due to excessive moisture at the recently constructed FMB building. The largest personal loss was sustained by Leonard Jennewein, Executive Secretary of the FMB. Philip Kaye, director of drama, lost his unfinished doctoral dissertation and research materials. Student grades were salvaged, and official records were saved in the vault.

Classes continued on schedule the following Monday morning, meeting in Science Hall and other available rooms on campus. The library was assigned to a basement room in Science Hall and administrative offices were moved to the first floor of the Music School.[6]

President Smith was in California at the time of the fire and could not be reached until Sunday afternoon.

> When Dr. Smith's plane touched down in Mitchell Monday morning he was met by Bradley Young, Chairman of the Board, and together they formulated plans to rebuild. The South Dakota Annual Conference of the Methodist Church met in special session in Science Hall and approved a campaign for funds. Dr. Robert Wagner, then pastor of First Methodist Church in Mitchell, volunteered to resign his pastorate and head the campaign. He directed a successful campaign, raising $175,000 from South Dakota Methodist churches, $175,000 from alumni, and $180,000 from the greater Mitchell community. This, along with the $195,000 insurance, enabled new College Hall to be built and equipped for $725,000 debt free.[7]

Ground-breaking ceremonies for the new College Hall were held on August 12, 1955. The cornerstone was laid on Blue and White Day (October 15) of the same year, with Senator Francis Case ('18) as speaker. On that same day ground was broken for a women's dormitory, Dayton Hall, which was financed in part with a loan from the Federal Housing and Urban Development Agency at 2.75 percent interest. A record crowd of alumni, students and friends attended the dedication of College Hall on Blue and White Day, October 20, 1956, with Bishop Edwin E. Voigt performing the ritual ceremony, and Dr. John O. Gross, executive secretary to the Board of Education of the Methodist Church, as the principal speaker.

Although the loss of College Hall had appeared as the ultimate calamity, it served to expedite Wesleyan's five-pronged program of development by coalescing its supporters. "The February tragedy sparked a new epoch in Wesleyan history," observed President Smith, "which is best expressed by Dakota Wesleyan University's adopted phrase, 'Out of disaster into a new day.'"[8]

Grace Bliss Dayton Hall, a women's dormitory named in honor of a liberally contributing alumna, was ready for occupancy for the 1957-1958 school year, with formal dedication ceremonies held on Blue and White Day on October 5, 1957. Graham Hall was remodeled for use as a men's dormitory that same summer. Investments in buildings, equipment and landscaping during the Smith administration totaled a million dollars. College enrollment grew 110 percent; the faculty was enlarged; salaries were raised 15 percent, and the operating budget was increased by one-third.[9] Having attained his goals, President Smith stepped aside to make room for a younger man.

Dr. Smith retained his relationships to the college as President Emeritus and director of alumnal affairs, a post he relinquished in 1969, terminating a career spanning thirty years at Dakota Wesleyan. Subsequently he worked as an archivist for the South Dakota Commission on Archives and History (Methodist). His faithful service to the University was recognized by the conferring of the honorary degree of Doctor of Humane Letters in 1959 and the renaming of College Hall as Matthew D. and Loretta Smith Hall in 1971. A portrait of President Smith was presented to Loretta Smith and Dakota Wesleyan by Mike Sougstad in 1982.

There was strong support for Robert Wagner, vice president in charge of the building program, to succeed Smith as president, but the election fell to Jack Jones Early. Early had been educated in the schools of his home state, receiving a doctorate in education from the University of Kentucky and a theological degree from the College of the Bible at Lexington. He occupied various Methodist pulpits in Kentucky, was vice president and dean at Iowa Wesleyan College, and was elected as President of Dakota Wesleyan University on June 2, 1958. He took office on the first of September.

"Dakota Wesleyan University — a tradition of quality, a commitment to the future." This was the slogan adopted for the seventy-fifth anniversary in 1960. Blue and White Day on October 24, 1959 carried the anniversary theme and was capped by a ceremony at which the original cornerstone of Merrill Hall was placed in a display case in the lobby of College Hall. Founders' Day, March 19, 1961, featured an honored son of Wesleyan, Senator Francis Case, as the convocation speaker, and a concert by the Dakota Wesleyan choir. There was also a huge anniversary cake topped with frosted replicas of Merrill Hall and the new College Hall. Final anniversary observances were made during commencement week, beginning May 12, 1961. Speakers included Bishop Edwin R. Garrison, baccalaureate; Dr. Francis D. Wilcox, commencement; and Thomas B. Leekey, alumni banquet. "Under the Wheel" by Hamlin Garland was presented by the drama department.

Dakota Wesleyan embarked on the last quarter of its first century on a note of optimism. The rains had returned to the parched plains. National post-war affluence and affirmation of democratic principles and the availability of federal funds ushered in the "golden age" of higher education in America in the late fifties and the sixties. Student enrollments climbed, campus facilities were expanded and educational programs enriched throughout the country and at Dakota Wesleyan. Without doubt, these fortuitous circumstances were a factor contributing to the impressive accomplishments of the Smith and Early administrations.

The "new look" on campus, begun with the construction of the new College Hall and Grace Bliss Dayton Hall during the Smith administration, was continued in the Early administration. Student housing became a top priority as enrollment increased. Government loans provided 50 percent of the funding ($225,000 at 3 percent interest) for Allen Hall, the new men's dormitory. A full loan ($370,000 at 3 percent interest) was procured for the east wing addition of the women's dormitory, and a 90 percent loan ($510,000 at 3 percent interest) for the Campus Center. Ground-breaking ceremonies for Allen Hall, named in honor of Harland Allen, a noted international economist and former student and benefactor of the college, were held on Blue and White Day, October 7, 1961. The building was completed in 1963. Shortly after the death of Dr. Allen, the Allen Hall government loan was discounted and paid from the residue of his now satisfied gift annuities.[10] Construction of the addition to Dayton Hall followed and it was ready for occupancy in 1966.

The campus "new look" was further enhanced by the erection of the Campus Center. This functional unit housed the dining hall and kitchen, a snack bar, the bookstore and campus post office, the student association and student publications offices, a faculty lounge, and social rooms for students. Wesleyan was also approved for a $500,000 government grant for the building of a fine arts center. This project was cancelled during the Huddleston administration.[11] Other campus improvements included the renovation of the laboratories and offices in Science Hall in the summer of 1960.

There was also a more cosmopolitan look on campus. Full-time enrollment soared from 391 in 1958 to a high of 714 in 1968. Part of the increase at the beginning of the sixties was the result of aggressive student recruitment by Lawrence "Pops" Harrison (dean of admissions 1959-1961). Harrison followed the approach of marketing education as a business commodity, which had gained national notoriety at Parsons College in Fairfield, Iowa. Of the 503 full-time enrollees of 1960-1961, 227 were freshmen, of whom 105 were from out-of-state, largely from eastern metropolitan areas.[12]

There was considerable strain when East met West at this Middle Border community. Although a number of the "outsiders" were excellent collegians, a sizable portion brought weak academic records from other schools, making Wesleyan a second-chance college. With approximately one-third of the enrollees admitted on probation, faculty morale flagged. Student retention was a problem. Theft and disorderly conduct became common in the dormitories. Downtown shoplifting and vandalism by Wesleyan students escalated, evoking swift disciplinary action by college officials. Blacks dating whites elicited racist responses, including a cross burning at Dayton Hall and the hanging in effigy of the college president in front of the *Daily Republic* office downtown. The newcomers also had grievances. There were complaints that recruiters had misrepresented the school's facilities and social programs and that prospective students had been promised scholarships and loans, only to be told they had none when they arrived.[13] A *Phreno Cosmian* article critical of the admissions operation brought threats of expulsion to the writer, Donald Messer ('63). His college career was spared termination by the staunch defense of students, including his roommate, Kent Millard (who consequently lost a five-hundred-dollar scholarship), and the unabashed support of Professor Leonard Jennewein, who threatened resignation.[14] With Harrison's departure, student recruitment was again more selective, focusing on South Dakota and the area states.

Two annual lecture series were inaugurated during Early's administration. The Stark Lectures, endowed by alumnus Franklin C. Stark ('37), were first given in 1959. Stark, an active Methodist layman and lawyer, was a charter member of the World Peace Through Law Center, founded in 1963. The first annual Family Life Conference, held in 1960, featured the renowned family expert, Evelyn Millis Duvall. The Conference was organized by Orlando Goering, head of sociology, and funded by a grant from Joe Messer of Watertown, South Dakota.

Having achieved his goals of increased student enrollment and the upgrading of professional standards and salary, President Early resigned in 1969 to become president of Pfeiffer College in Meisenheimer, North Carolina. He also left an impressive legacy of new buildings. These, however, carried a substantial capitol indebtedness which would burden future administrations.

Academic Program

There was no major revision in Dakota Wesleyan's curriculum upon Hilburn's departure in the spring of 1951. Academic courses were regrouped into three divisions in 1957-1958, namely the natural sciences and mathematics, the social sciences, and the humanities. General education courses constituted about 40 percent of the total number of hours required for a bachelor's degree. Preprofessional courses were offered in theology, law, medicine, and engineering.

Anticipation of a state law requiring a four-year certificate of all teachers led to the addition of a four-year course for elementary teachers and the discontinuation of the two-year course. Practice teaching became mandatory in 1955 and was done in cooperation with the Mitchell public school system. Miss Delores Leonard, president of the local chapter of the Future Teachers of America, was elected the first state president in 1954-1955.[15] A degree course in nursing, added to the curriculum in 1952, enabled students to qualify as supervisors or teachers in schools of nursing. The commerce department, now known as the department of business and economics, experienced steady growth under the capable leadership of Chester Rich and Wayne Williamson.

Enrollment in the School of Music plunged to a low of six during the war and remained small in the post-war era, resulting in the dropping of the Bachelor of Music Education degree. Among the music department's long-term teachers were Mary Woolsey, keyboard; Paul Schuerle, leader of the band; and William F. Kugel, vocal instructor and head of the department from 1949 until his death in 1963. Under Kugel's direction, the A Cappella Choir and smaller vocal ensembles such as the Wesleyan Singers and the Highlanders added much to the mood of worship and celebration at University and community events. Kugel's impact on the lives of students was depicted in the film, "Brother, My Song," filmed on campus in 1972 by Bruce Doggett (later known as Christopher Cain), assisted by Mel Dieken. It was premiered in Mitchell on November 6, 1973.

The consistently high quality of serious drama in this period can be attributed to the dynamic personality of Philip Kaye, director from 1947-1956, and the dedication of his successor, Mary Wing. Considerable emphasis was placed on religious drama, such as the original dramatization of "Elijah" by Mary Wing with the music setting by William Kugel, professor of music. The drama and music departments also collaborated in the production of operettas such as "The Unsinkable Molly Brown" and "Brigadoon."[16]

Layne Library holdings were limited due to fire and inadequate funding. This was compensated for in part by the use of a computer terminal and telephone line providing access to the nationwide automated library service consortium (OCLC). The library also had a learning resource center using audiovisual equipment and an outstanding collection of western and regional materials. Among the holdings of its Center for Frontier Studies were the Senator Francis Case Archives; the Jennewein Western Library, a gift of Mr. Jennewein and the class of 1912; the Badger Clark Collection; the Jedediah Smith Collection; and the Preacher Smith Collection.

The Francis Case collection of books, files, records, papers, and other items of personal property as selected by his widow, Mrs. Myrle G. Case, daughter Jane Case Commander, and brother Leland D. Case (ex '22), were given to Friends of the Middle Border to be used by FMB in connection with Dakota Wesleyan, "to continue with the ideas and ideals of Francis Case that popular government and cultural civilization start at the grass roots with the people."[17] Francis Case ('18) served in the U. S. House of Representatives from 1939 to 1951 and in the U.S. Senate from 1952 until his death in 1962. Richard Chenoweth, history professor, researched the Case papers for his doctoral dissertation, "Francis Case: A Political Biography," which was published in the 1978 *South Dakota Historical Collection.*

The memorabilia of another favorite son of Wesleyan, George McGovern ('46), was housed in the McGovern Room, dedicated in

1981. McGovern taught history and forensics at Wesleyan following his World War II service in the Air Force until 1953, when he resigned to enter politics. He served as U.S. representative from 1957 to 1961 and as U.S. senator from 1962 to 1980, and he was the Democratic nominee for the presidency in 1972.

Library resources also included the Joint Archives of the Dakota Wesleyan University and the Annual Conference of the South Dakota Methodist Church, located at the Conference Center adjacent to the campus.

Educators of merit given the rank of emeritus in recognition of years of service and devotion to Dakota Wesleyan University were Charles S. Dewey, chemistry; John V. "Jack" Leach, philosophy and religion; Florence White, foreign languages; Frank Wingfield, biology; and Mary Woolsey, music. Jesse Knox had been a familiar figure on campus since 1924 when he joined the teaching staff as professor of mathematics. He was college dean from 1951 until 1956, when he resigned due to age and ill health, having given thirty-two years of service to Wesleyan. He was followed by Thomas D. Henson, who held the office of dean for a record-breaking sixteen years. J. Leonard Jennewein came to Wesleyan in 1954 as executive secretary of the Friends of the Middle Border when Bob Pennington resigned from that post to give full time to teaching history and sociology. Jennewein, a walking storehouse of regional information, was a popular and effective English teacher (1955-1968) and brought prominence to the FMB as a museum and historical center.

Among the members of the staff who merit recognition for outstanding service were the following: Amelia "Billie" Gaetz, registrar; Harriet Houk, alumni office and placement; Vera Kilstrom, cashier; Wayne Jares, assistant business manager; Mildred Eyres, librarian; Elizabeth Kugel, Helen Thompson and Marie Forbes, library personnel; and Joe Wingert, Ed Sougstad and Cliff Gates, custodians. Jean Weston ('21) joined the Wesleyan staff in 1946 to supervise the kitchen and dining room. She served as dietician until her retirement in 1971, providing a quarter-century of "home cooked" meals at the college dining hall. A dining room in the Campus Center was named in her honor.

Student Life and Organizations

Turning to a consideration of extra-curricular activities and student life, we note that Dakota Wesleyan University maintained its leadership role in forensics. George McGovern was awarded a plaque in 1953 for having the best record of victories of any debate coach for a three-year period at the Rocky Mountain Speech Tournament. The 1952 speech squad won five out of seven events at the Pi Kappa Delta Sioux Province Tournament. A Wesleyan freshman, Barbara Rollins, won the distinction of being the first South Dakota coed to take first place in the national Pi Kappa Delta oratory contest. The seventy-fifth anniversary of Dakota Wesleyan was marked by another state championship in oratory, this one by Margaret Johnson.[18]

The Student Senate was the most representative organization on campus. Officers were elected by the entire student body. Boards under the jurisdiction of the Student Senate were the Recreation Board, the Calendar Board, the Athletic Board, the Social Committee, and the Religious Council. Student self-governing committees continued to take responsibility for dormitory regulations.[19]

Chapters of national honorary societies existent at Wesleyan in 1960 were the Phi Kappa Phi (scholastic), the Pi Kappa Delta (forensic), and the Theta Alpha Phi (dramatic). After a lapse of some years, Dakota Wesleyan was reinstated as the Alpha chapter of Sigma Tau Delta, the English fraternity. Among the numerous student groups were departmental and political clubs; the "W" Club for athletes who had been awarded monograms; the Ben Gals, a women's pep club; Circle K; the Aqua Sharks; and the Cosmopolitan Club, an intercultural group of foreign and American students.[20]

Student publications, the *Phreno Cosmian* and the *Tumbleweed*, continued to be published on a regular basis. The literary magazine, the *Prairie Wind*, previously under the auspices of the Writer's Club, became the special project of the creative writing class in 1959-1960 under the tutelage of Mary Weinkauf, professor of English and published author.

There were also twenty-five active alumni chapters throughout the United States. The Chicago chapter, the most active of these, funded the gateway at the entrance to the campus in 1948, memorializing the official merger of Black Hills College and Dakota Wesleyan University. They also raised twenty thousand dollars for the reconstruction of College Hall.

The sixties were both the best and worst of times on American campuses. Students enjoyed all the amenities that high enrollment and good cash flow could offer. Facilities were the best ever, and programs and activities gave a wide range of choice. This Elysium was shaken by the "hippie" generation whose confrontational protests against "the establishment" and America's involvement in the Vietnam war brought disruption and conflict to campuses throughout the nation. Yet even at the height of dissension, the campus atmosphere at Wesleyan was relatively calm and students tended to use established procedures to instigate change.

Compulsory chapel attendance became the focal point of the confrontation between the students and the administration at Dakota Wesleyan. Chapel attendance had not been required in the years immediately preceding the Early administration. A policy change enacted by the Board of Trustees took effect in the fall of 1962. It eliminated credit for chapel attendance and required all freshmen students and all students of following classes to attend the weekly chapel service. The 1966-1968 college catalog stated:

> Attendance at chapel is a requirement for continued attendance at Dakota Wesleyan University...Four unexcused absences from chapel is reason to deny enrollment in the following semester.

Separate services were provided for Roman Catholics. Alternatives were also provided for "those whose religious body forbids such attendance" and for requests to be excused for reason of conscience. In May 1966 Howard Bailey, campus minister and professor of philosophy, pointed out that student opinion ran 81 percent against mandatory chapel and suggested a compromise. Required worship, he added, is an obstacle to worship and makes it less meaningful.

The controversy intensified in February 1968 when local ministers and a group of community citizens brought pressure against the showing of the film "Candy" in a downtown theater. A complaint was drawn by the Deputy State's Attorney and brought to the University gymnasium, where it was signed by a gravel-voiced coach during a wrestling match. In consequence, the film was seized by the county sheriff and the theater owner arrested for exhibiting obscene material, a misdemeanor under South Dakota's obscenity law.

73

A great controversy ensued in the community which soon became polarized on the censorship issue. One minister found himself confronted with a "walkout" of about twenty-five college students from his Sunday morning worship service after he had stepped down from the pulpit to defend the film's removal. On the other hand, the campus minister found himself ostracized after denouncing censorship.[21]

On campus, the Candy controversy became part and parcel of the fight for individual freedom, accentuating a situation from which neither the president nor the campus minister could extricate himself. On March 16, 1969 the Executive Committee of the Board of Trustees passed President Early's recommendation that Bailey's contract not be renewed by a five-to-three vote. Student protest over Bailey's dismissal was tumultuous. Slogans proclaimed: "Academic Freedom Died Today. Why?" A petition for Bailey's reinstatement received over three hundred signatures from students and faculty. A one-year terminal contract was proffered, but Bailey chose to seek duty elsewhere.

Bailey's departure did not resolve the impasse over compulsory chapel attendance. On September 30, 1969 a disruption occurred at the regularly scheduled chapel program. The known participants were dismissed from the University but later reinstated. The following spring (1970) a questionnaire showed that a vast majority of the students opposed the rule. Subsequently, the Executive Committee of the Religious Life Council, which had been given authority over the matter, took steps to rescind mandatory chapel.

In view of Dakota Wesleyan's reputation for academic freedom and its ecumenical posture, the foment over the chapel issue cannot be explained in terms of revolt to narrow sectarian rule. Neither was the religious mix of the student body a significant factor. The struggle was basically the result of the Zeitgeist and of differing concepts of the chapel rule. The students perceived the chapel attendance rule as an infringement of their constitutional right of freedom of religion. The administration, on the other hand, exercised the right — some would say the obligation — of a private church-related institution to bring a spiritual dimension into the lives of its students. Attendance at chapel services had long been seen as a means to this end. In the years that followed, students were invited but not required to attend the weekly services.

Religious functions on campus were under the supervision of the director of religious life and the Religious Life Council. The latter, organized in 1962, was composed of student representatives from the residence halls, the Student Senate, the Methodist Student Movement, and two nominated by the director of religious life. Religious organizations included the Methodist Student Movement until 1970, when it was discontinued both nationally and locally; the Kappa Chi, composed of students interested in full-time Christian vocations; and the Catholic Students. A chapter of the Fellowship of Christian Athletes was founded in October 1966 by Gordon Fosness, basketball coach. Annual religious events included Religion in Life Week and the Franklin C. Stark lectures, most of which were religiously orientated.

Special efforts were made to meet the spiritual needs of the total student body, which became increasingly non-Methodist. The number of students indicating a Methodist preference dropped from 75 percent in 1929-1930 to 49 percent in the fall of 1960, with Catholics polling 20 percent and Lutherans 9 percent.[22]

Sports suffered none of the disruptions that plagued campus religious programs, but underwent a temporary slump. Wesleyan won no Conference championship in any sport during the decade of the fifties, but rebounded in the sixties. Star player for the cagers was Gordon Fosness ('57). Fosness closed his student career at Wesleyan as the highest-scoring college basketball player in South Dakota history, having racked up 1,805 points in four seasons, 1,409 of these in Conference competitions. He returned to Wesleyan as basketball coach in 1961. In 1963-64 he and Coach Gordon Zapp led the cagers into the first outright Conference championship and the first DWU team in the NAIA tourney in sixteen years.

Football recouped in 1965 under Coach Gordon Zapp. The score of 65-0 in Wesleyan's favor in a game with Jamestown, North Dakota, set a new record for Wesleyan. The 1965-66 season was declared "the most successful season (in terms of wins) in forty-nine years" and found the Tigers in second place in the final SDIC standing.[23]

An intercollegiate soccer team was formed in 1962 in response to demand by minority and international students, but competitors were hard to find. It was dropped from the SDIC schedule in the seventies. Wrestling, added to the intercollegiate sports in 1963, was dropped in 1971. Non-Conference sports included baseball, swimming, and golf. All women on campus were automatically members of the Women's Recreational Association. The coeds were active in field hockey, volleyball, basketball, and "powder puff football."

When not engrossed with books and studies, students spent time together at snack bars, taverns, and dorm rooms. The Tiger Lair in the new College Hall replaced the Rec Room as an informal gathering spot. Students enjoyed going to movies, dances at Morrow Gymnasium, parties, and ball games. They spent many hours planning and stuffing paper tissues into meshed wire to create elaborate floats for the Homecoming parade. Gathering to sing folk songs to the strum of Bill Bigger's guitar, dubbed a "hootenanny," became a popular pastime in the mid-sixties.

Memories of campus life came in bits and snatches: living three to a room in Dayton Hall...the Wesleyan Choir tour to San Francisco and Seattle...Sam Muyskens, 6'11", in the leading role of "Abe Lincoln in Illinois"...MSM summer work camp on Chicago's south side...card games between classes...the anthropology class uncovering a skeleton at Indian Head and posting an all-night vigil...the FMB campout at Ghost Hawk Camp on the Rosebud Reservation...May Day open house at Dayton Hall...the Bob Hope benefit performance at the Corn Palace...Dean Hartung in the dunking booth at the Spring Carnival...belly laughs at the W Club talent show...the annual Christmas tree decorated by the Circle K Club...Bengals...breakfasts before final exams.

A new spring rite evolved in 1963 around The-Little-Tree-That-Never-Grew. This small hackberry, about to be inundated by the waters of the Oahe dam, was brought to the campus from the banks of the Missouri. Students perpetuated the folklore that Indians had celebrated around the tree each spring when the first leaf appeared, blending innovation with tradition.

Financial Overview and Summary

Friends of Dakota Wesleyan University viewing the charred refuse of the old College Hall on February 12, 1955 could not have imagined the appearance of the campus a mere fifteen years later. The extent of institutional development in this brief period is reflected in a comparison of the following financial data for the fiscal years of 1950 and 1970:[24]

	1950	1970
Current fund/operating budget	$292,348	$1,532,724
Endowment fund	$554,414	$1,254,933
Buildings and grounds	$577,568	$4,118,210

Even when adjusted for inflation, these figures witness to salutary growth. Not shown in these statistics is the upgrading in the quality of instruction available to Dakota Wesleyan students because of better-trained teachers and improved teaching facilities. These had indeed been golden years in higher education at Wesleyan.

College Hall and Memory Lane (photograph taken between 1950 and 1955). College Hall was built in 1888 on the former site of Merrill Memorial Hall. The trees shown along Memory Lane were planted by the Class of 1943 in memory of DWU faculty and students who served in World War II. (Memory Lane was rededicated in 1989 by the Class of 1964.) The stone gateway which graces the north entrance to the campus was given to DWU around 1950 by the Chicago alumni chapter. The small stone at left reads "Sacrifice or Service;" the small stone at right reads "Class of 1950." The taller columns are shown in more detail below.

The College Hall fire on February 12, 1955 destroyed the entire building within a matter of hours.

The new College Hall, completed in 1956. The building was renamed Matthew D. and Loretta Smith Hall in 1971. Matthew Smith, a 1912 DWU alumnus, served as DWU's Dean in 1936-44, President in 1952-58, and Director of Alumni Affairs in 1958-69. He died on December 8, 1981 at the age of 90.

Completed in 1967, the Campus Center houses dining facilities, the bookstore, post office, snack shop, a recreational lounge, and student offices. The building was renamed the Gordon and Elsie Rollins Campus Center in 1987; Gordon Rollins served DWU for over 40 years as its business manager and vice president for finance.

An aerial view of the campus (from its northern side) in the 1970s. Music Hall is at bottom right. Other buildings shown (clockwise from top) are Stout Hall and Morrow Gymnasium, Grace Bliss Dayton Hall (completed in 1957), Science Hall, Smith Hall, Graham Hall, Allen Hall (completed in 1963), and the Rollins Campus Center.

Campus Life at Dakota Wesleyan University

Through the years, DWU students have devoted themselves to the serious business of academic growth through work in the classroom...

A business administration classroom in Smith Hall.

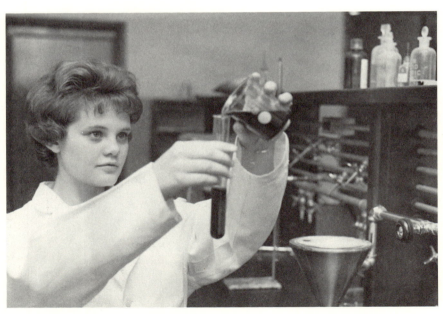

A student conducts an experiment in the Science Hall chemistry laboratory.

...and outside preparation in the library and residence halls.

A scene from Layne Library.

Male students studying in the Allen Hall lounge.

In addition to studies, students took time out to enjoy meals...

A dining room scene from 1959.

Jean Weston, a 1921 alumna, served as DWU's dietician from 1946 to 1971. The Weston Private Dining Room in the Rollins Campus Center is named in her honor.

...and tend to the other "essential details" of daily living.

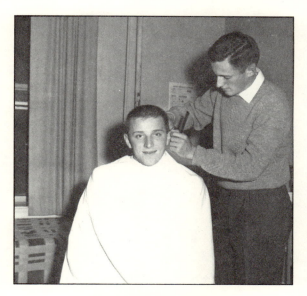

A haircut in Graham Hall.

Students getting their mail at the campus post office.

Free time was often spent socializing...

Female students gathering in the residence hall lounge.

Students pose behind the engraved rock which was given as a memorial from the Class of 1912.

...and enjoying athletic and campus events.

A scene from the 1965 Water Show held in the pool at Morrow Gymnasium.

The Christen Family Recreation/Wellness Center was completed in 1986. It includes a central arena for basketball and volleyball, as well as racquetball courts, exercise and weight rooms, a classroom, offices, and a lounge. The facility was made possible by a million-dollar gift from Paul and Donna Christen, and it is named after their parents.

Throughout its 100-year history, Dakota Wesleyan University has enhanced its academic, physical, and social offerings by providing students with opportunities for spiritual growth.

Shandorf Chapel (formerly known as the Upper Room), a small chapel on the fifth floor of Smith Hall, is named after Fred and Mary Cass Shandorf, who funded its renovations in 1977.

Chapter VI

The Quest for Excellence: 1969-1985

Administrative Highlights

Coming to Mitchell in the spring of 1969, President Robert Huddleston and family were the first to occupy the new president's residence, also known as the Fredericks' Place, at 1331 S. Minnesota. It was funded by the estate gift of George Fredericks, a former Mitchell mayor and member of the college Board. Dr. Huddleston, an ordained United Methodist minister, had most recently served as vice president for development at Westminister College in Salt Lake City, Utah.

Dr. Huddleston's repute as a skilled fund-raiser was a factor in his selection for the presidency. The years of plenty had passed. Enrollment was on the downward curve and general receipts dropped proportionately. Empty dormitory rooms, built to accommodate the large student population of the sixties, made loan repayments burdensome. However, Huddleston encountered early difficulty when he suggested that the college might need to move away from its historic ties with the United Methodist Church in order to strengthen its support for the future.[1] In the fall of 1970 a group of young United Methodist pastors, concerned for the well-being of their Alma Mater, engaged in a study and warned of an impending "crisis of confidence." Their critical report on the status of the college, penned by Dr. Donald Messer, was published in The *Plumb Line*, a church renewal paper sponsored by United Methodist clergy in South Dakota going by the acronym AMOS (Associated Ministries of Support). After publication of the article, they were summoned to meet with the Executive Committee of the Board of Trustees of Dakota Wesleyan University to defend their report.[2] President Huddleston was given a vote of confidence at the fall (1970) meeting of the Board. The Cummerford Corporation, a firm of fund-raising consultants, was hired at the same meeting to make a preliminary survey as to the feasibility of a campaign to cover the accumulated deficit.

By the spring of 1971 the operating deficit had ballooned to $180,000. Moreover, the Cummerford Corporation, in their report to the Board, stated that many in the constituency had lost confidence in the president, which made the outlook for a financial campaign unfavorable as long as he remained in office.[3] Huddleston's resignation, effective within three days, was accepted at the same meeting. The Cummerford Corporation was hired to proceed with a financial drive and an interim committee was appointed to handle the affairs of the University. Its members were Boyd Knox, Chairman of the Board; Gordon Rollins, treasurer and business manager; and an elected representative.[4] Dr. Robert H. Wagner, pastor of the First United Methodist Church of Sioux Falls, was selected as interim president for a period of three months beginning March 9, 1971.[5]

Once again, as in 1955, Wagner stepped forward to play a critical leadership role, reestablishing a feeling of confidence within the school and its constituency. Operating costs were pared and debt reduction achieved by such one-time transactions as the sale of college real estate and the reinvestment of endowment funds. The fund-raising campaign netted $300,000. Emphasis was placed on student recruitment with forty freshmen awards of $250, the amount lost on one empty dormitory bed, as incentive.[6] By November 1971 an investigating committee could report that finances were in hand, giving special recognition to Gordon Rollins, "a very capable and dedicated business manager..."[7]

Dr. Wagner proved himself a capable interim president and was generally favored as the person to be selected as the next president of Dakota Wesleyan. Among the five persons interviewed for the position was Dr. Donald Messer, who had entered his name as a candidate at the urging of his friend and mentor, Robert Wagner, on the day after Huddleston's departure.

> I was the least experienced and had offered to withdraw from the competition a week before the vote, but had been encouraged to go through the experience and let the Board make the final decision. No one, including myself, expected that I would be chosen. But much to the consternation of the Board, the search committee by a three to two vote urged my election. At what apparently was a tumultuous Board meeting, after that recommendation was made, a final vote confirmed me as president by a 14-12 vote. Bonnie and I were shocked beyond words.

When the announcement was made the next day at the Corn Palace during Commencement, there was stunned silence.[8]

Dr. Messer was the first native South Dakotan and the second alumnus to hold the office of president of Dakota Wesleyan. Born and reared at Kimball, he received his BA from Wesleyan in 1963, graduated magna cum laude from the Boston School of Theology in 1966, and received his doctorate from Boston University in 1969. He was serving as assistant pastor at the First United Methodist Church in Sioux Falls at the time of his election in May 1971.

President Messer faced a three-pronged challenge: restoring a strong relationship with the church constituency, stabilizing enrollment, and eliminating the operational deficit.[9] Reversing the trend of the two previous administrations, Messer reaffirmed the regional and denominational roots of Dakota Wesleyan and enhanced church-school relationships, thereby rallying the laity and pastors of the supporting Conference to his support. Fiscal support of the South Dakota Annual Conference, in the form of unrestricted gifts, rose from $60,000 to $136,000 annually, giving South Dakota Methodists the distinction of having the highest per capita giving for higher education in the entire denomination.[10] Enrollment climbed steadily through 1977, with 70 percent of the 1980-81 student body from South Dakota, plus 13 percent from the surrounding states.

Committed to academic freedom and quality education, the Messer administration upgraded the educational and administrative staff and course offerings. The percentage of full-time faculty holding doctorate degrees rose from 12 percent in 1970 to 43 percent in 1974. The quality of the academic program was attested to by the North Central Association of Colleges and Universities' unqualified accreditation of Dakota Wesleyan for the maximum ten-year period, without review, in 1977.[11]

Reflecting on the years of his presidency, Dr. Messer wrote:

Education and fund-raising didn't function in a political vacuum. Quite to the contrary, it was a time of great ferment as we struggled to make operational the achievements of the civil rights struggle...Women's rights were coming to the forefront of our agendas. Controversy was unending in regard to the Vietnam War. Then the Watergate scandal emerged.

While many small rural colleges might have escaped the political turmoil and consequences of these developments, Dakota Wesleyan could not. Our best-known graduate and former faculty member was George S. McGovern, a United States senator from South Dakota and leading opponent of the Vietnam War. In 1972 he was nominated by the Democrats as their candidate for President. Throughout 1971 and 1972 DWU received an endless stream of journalists from the major newspapers...they came to the campus for interviews and to see where McGovern had emerged.

...Besides the publicity involved, there was considerable tension behind the scenes working with the Secret Service. At one point Eleanor McGovern's life was threatened, and I had to search Wesleyan's records as they believed the person making the threats had been a DWU student...[12]

McGovern made his last campaign speech to an enormous crowd on the Dakota Wesleyan campus on election day in November 1972. "It marked the end of a very unusual and exciting period in the school's history as the college was thrust to the forefront of public life."[13]

In another incident, the growing involvement of government in the affairs of private institutions resulted in charges of sex discrimination in the hosting of Girls State, brought against Dakota Wesleyan University by the South Dakota Division of Human Rights. The irony of this action was expressed by a past governor of Girls State who released the following statement to the newspapers:

Back in the 1940's when the South Dakota Auxiliary decided to conduct a South Dakota Girls State they needed a campus to use. Prejudice ran high against females and the Auxiliary. The only campus in the state that would allow the use of its facilities was Dakota Wesleyan University in Mitchell...Thus in 1947 Girls State began in Mitchell and has been held there ever since...The Auxiliary's pride and dedication to Dakota Wesleyan runs deep.[14]

The charge was eventually dropped.

The decade of the seventies was marked by an oil crunch coupled with a major national recession and double-digit inflation. It was a period for conservation rather than expansion. No major building projects were undertaken during these years, but several were envisioned, including a new sports complex and a centennial chapel/fine arts building. Fund-raising for the latter, initiated by President Messer shortly before his departure from Wesleyan, had been endorsed by the South Dakota Annual Conference. The project was temporarily put on hold by the following administration.

92

On campus the word from William Houk, professor of biology and chairman of the University Energy Task Force, was "insulate, insulate." Science Hall was renovated in 1976. In the process the stained glass windows in the chapel that had been hidden for decades were uncovered. Lights to illuminate them were acquired through the Gold Hauser (1899) estate.[15] Dedication of the Drs. Kenneth and Marian Sherman Chapel/Theater was held May 5, 1977. Minor renovations included the redecoration of the small chapel on the fifth floor of Smith Hall, the special project of Fred and Mary Cass Shandorf, for whom it was named. Its stained glass windows were crafted by Minnietta Green Millard ('63). A campus carillon, the gift of Boyd Knox, Chairman of the Board of Trustees from 1969-1981, was given in memory of his wife Beverly and was dedicated at commencement in 1977. Mr. Knox also donated funds to remodel the East Private Dining Room at the Campus Center. The school also received portraits of two noted alumni, namely Francis Case and George McGovern, gifts from Marilyn Sunderman, an alumna and renowned artist.

Dr. Messer, who had been South Dakota's youngest college president at the time of his inauguration, enjoyed his status as the state's senior college administrator at the time of his resignation in the spring of 1981. Personal honors that had come to him included the presentation of the Key to the City by Mitchell's mayor, an honorary doctorate degree from Dakota Wesleyan University, and being named Outstanding Young Man for 1975, one of ten persons selected nationwide by the U. S. Jaycees. The years of his incumbency were marked by a strengthening of church/school ties, academic upgrading and fiscal stability. The endowment fund grew to be the largest among South Dakota private colleges. Messer resigned effective June 26, 1881 to accept the presidency of Iliff School of Theology. Dr. James B. Beddow was elected to fill the vacancy at Wesleyan.

Dr. Beddow was the second native son of South Dakota and the second lay person to serve as president of Dakota Wesleyan University. Born at Huron, he attended high school at Woonsocket, graduated from the University of South Dakota, and received his doctorate from the University of Oklahoma in 1969. Following two years as a captain in the United States Army, Dr. Beddow launched his career as an educator, serving as academic vice president and associate professor of history at Phillips University. He was president of the Colleges of Mid-America from 1976-1979, at which time

93

he accepted the position of vice president for institutional advancement at Sioux Falls College in Sioux Falls, South Dakota. While at Sioux Falls College he was a member of Wesleyan's special task force to consider ways that the South Dakota Annual Conference might be involved in a major campaign for the building of a centennial chapel. Beddow was elected president of Dakota Wesleyan University by unanimous ballot in the spring of 1981.

A young and energetic man, President Beddow was well-suited to the challenges of the eighties. Student enrollment had begun a downward trend in the late seventies, reflecting the dwindling number of high school graduates. Federal assistance in the form of Title programs, student grants and loan programs were slashed by Reaganomics. Furthermore, private schools were put at a disadvantage in student recruitment by the widening gap between tuition costs at private and public schools. Despite these obstacles, Dakota Wesleyan moved forward on all fronts.

After a year-long consultation with the college's constituency, the Beddow administration shifted priorities for the centennial campaign. The proposed chapel/fine arts building was postponed in order to focus on more pressing needs. A three-year campaign, the Agenda for Excellence, was approved by the Board of Trustees at its spring 1983 meeting. More than just a fund-raising project, the Agenda for Excellence hoped to involve the nationwide constituency in the college's second century through providing operating support, increased endowment funds, and construction of a new recreation/wellness center to improve the quality of campus life. Morrow Gymnasium had fallen into disrepair and no longer met student needs. A portion of the building had been declared structurally unsafe, necessitating the closing of the swimming pool.

The Agenda for Excellence campaign for $6,200,000 was launched at the Corn Palace on April 6, 1984 with the premiere of the film, "At the Edge," produced by John Kindschuh of Pictorial Publishers, Inc. A full house was on hand to hear the keynote speaker, former Mitchellite Joe Robbie, owner of the Miami Dolphins. Ground-breaking ceremonies for the new recreational facility took place in November 1984. The naming and cornerstone ceremony was held on April 17, 1985 as part of Dakota Wesleyan's centennial observances. The new health center was made possible by the commitment of one million dollars by Paul and Donna Christen to the Agenda for Excellence Campaign. It was named the Chris-

94

ten Family Recreation/Wellness Center in honor of the Christens' parents, Philip and Ruby Christen and Herbert and Gyda Starr.

The Recreation/Wellness Center was planned to meet the recreational and health needs of the entire college community. It included a central arena for basketball, volleyball and tennis, with a jogging track encircling the court area. Additional features were racquetball courts, exercise and weight rooms, a conference room, classroom, offices and lounge.

Other campus improvements during the pre-centennial years of the Beddow administration included the renovation of the biology laboratories in Science Hall in 1984. The interior of Music Hall was remodeled the same year. It now housed the media/publications offices in the basement, admissions and financial aid on first floor, and music offices and practice rooms on the second and third floors.

Academic Program

Dakota Wesleyan University's historic dual function as a liberal arts college and an occupational training provider gave it flexibility in the reconstruction of its educational program to meet the needs of the post-Vietnam War era. New courses for women and minorities reflected the Great Society's emphasis on equal opportunity. Computer technology spawned new occupational careers and exponentially increased the pool of information available to scholars. Non-traditional students (those over twenty-three years of age) flooded campuses, seeking intellectual enrichment and honing their skills for the job market.

Curricular changes to meet the new conditions entailed vision and effort. As dean Thomas Henson reported to his colleagues in 1970:

> It has been said that changing the curriculum is like moving the cemetery. The dead ideas of the past are often well and beautifully preserved, and present great problems to persons wanting to change...[16]

A core curriculum stressing interdisciplinary studies and the discussion of current challenges and conflicts supplanted the general education requirement in the 4-1-4 calendar adopted in 1970-1971. Most features of this smorgasbord system, which included individualized majors, were dropped by the end of the decade when general education requirements for the baccalaureate degree were reinstated. The one-month interim allowed for study on and off campus, including travel study programs abroad. The first of these took students to the Instituto Allende in Mexico to study art, history and language and to London to study Shakespearean drama. Interim studies have remained a popular feature of the school calendar, with twenty-eight course offerings for the 1986 interim.

The trend toward short-term, utilitarian courses resulted in a plethora of associate degree programs. Whereas all the graduates of 1963 received baccalaureate degrees, 36 percent of the graduates of 1983 received associate degrees. Two-year programs included accounting, criminal justice, office management, monetary and bank management, computer science, agri-business, allied health services, and numerous others. The largest of these was the nursing program, which received national accreditation. Launched in 1972 when the Methodist Hospital School of Nursing closed, it qualified graduates to write the National Council Licensing Examination for licensure as a registered nurse. The program was under the supervision of Faith Hubbard, associate professor and head of the department of nursing since 1973. The first capping ceremony was held on April 26, 1975 with Dr. Mildred Montag, founder of the Associate Degree Program in Nursing in the United States, as speaker. A Black Hills satellite nursing program was begun in 1981. Whereas many two-year course offerings were of short duration, nursing remained a popular choice.

A shift in student career choices brought a reshuffling of position among the long-established auxiliary departments, namely teacher training, commerce and music. Teacher training (the department of education), which had led in student enrollment since the founding of the University, was surpassed by commerce (the department of business administration and economics). In a landmark decision, the once vibrant School of Music was phased out by the discontinuation of music majors and minors. A fine arts major combining music, studio art, communication, and theatre was offered beginning in 1985-1986. Strong interest in the dramatic arts continued with Darryl Patten, known around campus circles as "Mr. Theatre," as director. In addition to three or four drama productions a year, the theatre program included interims in London and participation in the American College Theatre Festivals. Continuing a proud tradition, Dakota Wesleyan's seventy-fifth anniversary was marked by a state championship in oratory by Margaret

Johnson. Dale Nelson participated in the 1980 National Forensics Association competition.

New four-year degree programs included health, physical education and recreation (HYPER); American Indian studies, including Lakota, with David J. Mathieu, coordinator; and an accredited social work program. The latter, initiated by Bonnie Messer, was later headed by Virginia "Ginger" Wintemute ('65). Changes in accreditation requirements led to the replacement of the social work program by a human services degree in 1984. Pre-professional courses were offered in medicine, engineering, law, and theology.

Courses and credits were also designed for the non-traditional students who accounted for 48.6 percent of the total enrollment in the fall of 1983.[17] A concerted effort to attract and serve South Dakota's Native American population was begun in the early seventies. By 1984 their number had grown to thirty-five, constituting about 8 percent of the enrollees. Because the 1970s were times of considerable social and political turmoil, including the rise of a militant Native American movement, the Wounded Knee crisis, and various takeovers, Dakota Wesleyan's efforts in this area were not achieved without some resistance from the white community.[18] Another venture in multi-cultural education was the establishment of an annual exchange program between Dakota Wesleyan University and Koka Women's Institute of Kyoto, Japan. This program, initiated by Darryl Patten, brought twenty students and three teachers from Koka Institute to Mitchell in the summer of 1982. Alternating with Koka Institute, Wesleyan students and teachers have traveled to Japan for cultural and language studies every other year, beginning in 1983.[19]

Creative teaching took studies beyond the classroom. Dr. Merlin Gramm ('58), who chaired the Professional Advisory Committee for the Study of Correctional Policies and Programs in South Dakota, joined the Wesleyan staff as professor of education and psychology in 1966. One of his innovative programs on campus was the Attention Center. Working in cooperation with local police and the county judge, the Attention Center gave troubled juveniles an alternative to detention in the county jail. Students in a special psychology class provided supervision of the young men, who attended classes, ate at the dining hall, and slept in dormitories while on campus. The Center won high points from local law officers who credited it for reducing delinquency in Mitchell.

In another example of innovative teaching by Wesleyan faculty, Dr. Lesta Turchen, professor of history and political science, and Dr. James McLaird, associate professor of history, arranged for Wesleyan students to participate in the archeological excavation of prehistoric Mitchell Village, thereby gaining field experience in regional archeology and anthropology. Classroom learning was combined with social service when thirty-eight students participated in activity therapy programs for the elderly in nursing and retirement homes of the area. In one month alone this program touched the lives of eight hundred senior citizens.

Of the many teachers and staff persons of merit who have not already been mentioned, we list a few more: Dr. Loran Hills, professor of chemistry, recognized for his implementation of the computer science program; Dr. Robert Tatina, associate professor of biology; Rochelle Von Eye, recipient of the 1984 Presidential Award for Excellence in science and mathematics teaching; Dr. David Mitchell, associate professor of sociology and economics and director of institutional research and planning since 1973; Dr. Michael Turchen, professor and head of the department of communication and theatre since 1972; Marvin Miller, professor of religion and philosophy; Fay Barr-Hartung, the first female dean of students; Helen Trimble, the first female vice president of academic affairs; Dr. Milton Kudlacek, professor of art since 1958; Michael J. Wright, instructor in library science and director of learning resources; John Guy, manager of the Campus Center; Evalyn Sougstad Claggett, serving from 1972 to 1984 in the public relations, Title III, and admissions offices; and Linda Burnham, secretary *par excellence* to four presidents — Early, Huddleston, Messer and Beddow. Bonnie Messer organized the first DWU preschool and was the first president's wife to hold a teaching position at Dakota Wesleyan. In another first for presidents' wives, Jean Beddow served as a representative in the State Legislature at Pierre.

One of the giants on the Wesleyan staff was Gordon Rollins, treasurer and business manager from 1946 to 1975. His expertise in the handling of institutional finances carried Dakota Wesleyan through numerous crises and was acknowledged by the United Methodist Survey Committee of the Board of Education in a 1970 report which stated, "An excellent job of financial management is being done at Dakota Wesleyan University. Few institutions get more for their money than here."[20] Following his resignation as business manager, Rollins served as vice president for finance, bringing his term of service at Wesleyan to nearly forty years. The Campus Center was renamed the Gordon and Elsie Rollins Campus Center in 1987 to honor the Rollins.

Among the educational trends of this period was the increasing reliance on testing and an expansion of student services.

> The early deans' positions gradually emerged in the 1960's and 1970's into a service orientation as they became managers of an ever-expanding variety of programs and services in behalf of students — health service, food service, residential service, career service, placement service, and so on. Student personnel administrators of the 1980's recognize that they must be much more than simply "controllers of behavior" or "managers of service."[21]

Their new role, according to President Beddow, was that of educators. A comprehensive counseling system, centered at Graham Hall and directed through the student services and academic affairs offices, assigned an academic and a peer advisor to each student. Special Services, a government program, offered assistance to first-generation college students and those with physical handicaps or learning disabilities. Forty-four students and twenty-three tutors were engaged in this program in 1984.[22]

The technological revolution in communications brought major changes to Layne Library in the early eighties. Library catalog records were converted to data processing machines. A security system was installed to prevent book loss. Access to educational materials was augmented by the installation of a satellite TV receiver and by participation in the OLCC (On Line College Center) computer network. Such networks were a boon to libraries of small, geographically isolated colleges and exemplified the best of the technological impact on the educational scene.

Student Life and Organizations

When Dakota Wesleyan University first opened its doors in the late nineteenth century, it served a very young student population, many of whom were enrolled in the Academy and lived in College Hall. Increasingly in the twentieth century, the student body consisted of high school graduates, most of whom lived on campus, creating a cohesive college community. The demography of the student body changed again in the latter half of that century. President Beddow, in comments to the Wesleyan faculty and staff in the fall of

1984, stated that the student body had changed "from a four-year residential population to a fragmented population of traditional, non-traditional, and two- and four-year students with fewer and fewer living on campus."[23] There was an expressed need for more on-campus students to revitalize the DWU experience for traditional students.

New student organizations reflected the increase of minorities and married students. Among them were the Afro-American Center, Oyate Ho Waste (Native American), and the Wesleyannes (student wives). In the winter of 1984 the Student Senate appropriated $3,400 to the Methodist Hospital Child Care Center. These funds were to assist twenty-one parent-students at the college.[24]

Among the campus publications, the official student paper, the *Phreno Cosmian;* the annual yearbook, the *Tumbleweed;* and the Sigma Tau Delta literary publication, *Prairie Wind*, continued to be issued on a regular basis. In addition, there were two new publications. The *Tiger Tribune*, published by the dean of student services, functioned as a bulletin board of campus happenings. The *Dakota Wesleyan World* served as an alumni communication tool.

The views and participation of students in administrative decisions and governing policies were fostered by the Messer and Beddow administrations. Student life became less regulated by outmoded codes of conduct, but not without a struggle. The headline STUDENTS CHALLENGE SYSTEM AND CONVENTIONAL METHODS stood out in bold black print in the 1970 *Tumbleweed*. Challenged were dress codes, dormitory regulations, censorship, and compulsory chapel. Throughout the sixties, slacks, shorts, and bare feet were taboo in classrooms, library, dining hall, and the Campus Center, except on Saturdays. The noon meal on Sundays was a dress-up affair with heels and dresses or suits for women and coats and ties for men. This was the mini-skirt era and leg warmers were not "in." Linda Burnham recalled, as the most difficult task in her many years in the president's office, having to tell a student aide who came to work wearing slacks on a sub-zero morning that she had to go home and change. In time blue jeans became the unofficial school uniform. The 1973-1974 dress code simply stated, "Appropriate and comfortable dress is encouraged on the Wesleyan campus."

Students presented the following demands to dean Bob Ruth in 1969: off-campus housing, open door visitation in dormitories, no required chapel, permission to have cigarette vending machines on campus, and permission to have beer in dormitories. There was considerable hassling and eventual compromise on these issues. Off-campus housing privileges were granted only to students over twenty-three. The decision was economic: empty dormitory rooms did not facilitate loan repayments. Dormitory room visitation with students of the opposite sex was allowed during approved hours — noon to midnight on weekdays; noon to 1:00 a.m. on weekends. The student lounge at the Campus Center was opened on a twenty-four hour basis. Dormitory hours and sign-outs for residents were dropped. A coed dormitory open to upperclassmen was first set up on the upper floors of Graham Hall and later at Dayton Hall. Students were granted representation on the Board of Trustees, and a statement on student rights and responsibilities was worked out by a joint student-faculty committee.

The Student Senate continued to play a vital role in campus programming, managing (in 1985) a budget of more than $35,000 that funded student activities and publications and other functions. Student Association fees provided its main money source. Special projects included the remodeling of the Cultural Center, the refurbishing and outfitting of the Game Room, and the erection of pole lights around the campus.[25]

Student activities were planned by the Religious Life Council (RLC), the Student Activities Board (SAB), and the Recreational Sports Board. One year's calendar offered special movies, a fast for world hunger, and a "Black Hills invasion," which included skiing and relaxation at Storm Mountain Retreat Center, sponsored by the RLC. Dances, movies, and roller skating were on the SAB's social agenda. The Recreational Sports Board organized such events as 3-on-3 basketball, intramural basketball, and Homecoming softball tournaments. Valentine's Day called for a Sweethearts' Dance, and Indian Awareness Days were observed with a pow wow.

The supervision of religious functions on campus continued to lie in the hands of the campus minister and the Religious Life Council. In addition, there were numerous small organized religious groups with differing purposes and memberships. These included, at one time or another, the Kappi Chi, the Fellowship of Christian Athletes, Chrysalis, the Catholic Fellowship, Lutheran Students, and Brothers and Sisters in Christ (BASIC). The Social Concerns Task Force dealt with such issues as hunger, nuclear disarmament, and racism. Among its projects were dances for dystrophy and the raising of $3,300 for world hunger during the years of David Heetland's campus ministry (1977-1980). Student Outreach Teams, sponsored by the Religious Life Council, led Sunday morning worships and worked with church youth groups throughout the Dakotas. Duane Wilterdink served as campus minister beginning in 1980.

A Religious Life Program Review in spring 1985 reported the religious preferences of the Wesleyan student body as follows:[26]

Roman Catholic	23%	136 students
United Methodist	21%	125 students
Lutheran	17%	99 students
Baptist	4%	20 students
Episcopal	4%	20 students
Presbyterian	3%	17 students
Others	12%	68 students
Not indicated	18%	106 students

An average of fifty students and 10 percent of the faculty attended the weekly voluntary chapel. Religious life programming included eight small groups (four student outreach, four fellowship). The programs were student-led with the help and oversight of the campus minister. The average weekly contact for all small groups, chapel, and counseling was from 125 to 150 persons (some students participated in more than one group event). The combined religion and philosophy department, with one-and-one-half faculty, offered a wide variety of courses for a major and minor. One course in religion/philosophy was required for general education. Representative of catalog statements of institutional aims were the following:

To ensure an atmosphere conducive to freedom of thought...

To provide curriculum offerings and career opportunities which meet human needs and emphasize Christian service.

To encourage an awareness of the holistic nature of truth: stressing religious values which enable persons to think, act critically, creatively, and responsibly in an ever-changing world.

In contrast to Wesleyan's early days when the "Y"s were campus giants, overt involvement with religious matters appears to have waned. If so, various factors abetted the trend: the growing religious and cultural diversity of the student body; the inroads of secularism; an altered concept of Christian vocation. Whereas earlier student generations tended to think of a religious life as devoted to the ministry or the mission field, later student generations perceived of religion as permeating all vocations. A wholesome school atmosphere and a faculty and administration committed to Christian principles continued to characterize Dakota Wesleyan.

Sports continued to evoke enthusiastic school spirit. Dakota Wesleyan's Athletic Hall of Fame was initiated in the fall of 1977 to give recognition to athletes, coaches, and others who have been significantly involved in the school's athletic program. Charter members, inducted at the Blue and White Day banquet on October 14, 1977, were Matthew D. Smith, Mark Payne, Kenneth Harkness, Richard D. Dougherty, M. A. Hoellwarth, Glenn Draisey, and Gordon Fosness. An athletic scholarship of $15,000 was established in Dougherty's name by Galvin Walker, Fred Scallin, Zack Wipf, Lyle Nelson, Sam Weller, Harold Rietz, and others. Zack Wipf, who played football for five years in the twenties, was added to the roster in 1979 and also set up a scholarship of $15,000 in his own name.

Emphasis on equal opportunity and funds available through the Title IX program brought a boost to the women's physical education program in the seventies, which included intercollegiate volleyball, basketball, softball, track, and cross country. Coach Gordon Fosness and President Messer were instrumental in creating a women's division in the South Dakota Intercollegiate Conference (SDIC). The college was a member of the National Association of Intercollegiate Athletics (NAIA) Women's Division, which was organized in 1980. The Lady Tigers won the SDIC competition in basketball in 1980 and competed in one softball NAIA playoff.

Men's baseball, which had had a rather spasmodic existence, became an intercollegiate sport in 1981. Tennis had its devotees, with Paul Nielsen winning the SDIC singles championship in 1980. On the gridiron, the 1976 football team, with Ron Parks as coach, emerged as SDIC champions. A rare "double" was achieved in 1977 when the Tigers were named league champions in both football and basketball. With the glory came agony when Todd Wieczorek died of injuries received in football in the fall of 1980.

The Wesleyan Tigers continued their leading role in basketball. A record was set in 1978-79 when the cagers won twenty-four straight games, the most consecutive victories ever by a South Dakota team. Wesleyan's outstanding record in basketball was attributable in large part to "Gordie" Fosness, "the winningest [basketball] coach in the school's history." During his twenty-two years as coach he led the Wesleyan Tigers to 351 victories, ten SDIC championships, fourteen Holiday Tournament titles, and thirteen NAIA playoffs, of which two teams competed in the NAIA national tournament. He was named South Dakota College Coach of the Year in 1967 and 1979 and has been inducted into the Dakota Wesleyan University, the SDIC, and the NAIA Athletic Halls of Fame. Fosness was concerned with the total well-being of his players both on and off the basketball floor, organizing the Fellowship of Christian Athletes at Wesleyan in 1967. He stepped down as head basketball coach in 1983 and took the position of associate of development.

The DWU Tigers continued to score well under Coach Jim Martin, whose 16-10 overall record and 7-3 record in the SDIC captured the SDIC crown in 1985. Alan Miller, one of DWU's outstanding players, scored an average of 32.5 points per game, the best nationally in a collegiate division, and was named NAIA All-American. Miller also set the South Dakota career scoring record with 2,920 points and the state single-game mark with 55 points in a double-overtime victory over Sioux Falls College.[27] A tradition lives on.

Financial Overview and Summary

Dakota Wesleyan University received outstanding support from its main sources of income during the years 1971 to 1985. These included the South Dakota Conference of the Methodist Church, over six thousand alumni scattered around the globe, and the Mitchell community. Government support through title programs and student grants and loans peaked in the seventies. The most prominent of these was Title III, Basic Institutional Development Program, funded by the Department of Health, Education and Welfare. Wesleyan was also the recipient of a Bush Foundation challenge grant and a $310,000 challenge grant from the National Endowment for the Humanities in 1980.

With the tapering off of so-called "soft monies" under Reaganomics, Dakota Wesleyan tightened its belt and continued to operate on a balanced budget while increasing its operating budget and endowment fund. A number of scholarships were established to assist students in meeting the high cost of a private college education. These included the United Methodist Scholarship, a matching program for United Methodist churches; the Randall Scholars Program, a corporate gift from Randall Stores, Inc.

in memory of F. Dwain "Doc" Randall; the Presidential Scholarships; and four endowed scholarships by Drs. Kenneth E. and Marian M. Sherman.

The thrust toward economic viability and academic excellence begun in the 1970s moved forward with the Agenda for Excellence in the 1980s. Dakota Wesleyan conducted an intensive analysis of its academic program in order to provide the best possible preparation for the students who would be the leaders of the twenty-first century. At a time when red ink and a lack of students was putting other colleges of the area on the auction block, Dakota Wesleyan looked toward the continuation of its educational thrust into its second century.

Centennial Observances

Dakota Wesleyan University's centennial observances commenced on April 25, 1985 with the Stark Lectures. Featured speakers for the theme, "Peace and Public Policy," were Franklin C. Stark ('37), a prominent lawyer and active United Methodist layman, and George S. McGovern ('46) former US senator, director of the United States Food for Peace Program under President Kennedy, and Democratic nominee for President in 1972. A Centennial/Heritage Banquet was held at the Corn Palace on the evening of April 26, with Dr. Donald Messer ('68), president of Iliff School of Theology and former president of DWU, as speaker. A focal point of Centennial activities was the naming and cornerstone ceremony for the Recreation/Wellness Center on Saturday, April 27.

Alumni events were also scheduled for Saturday, April 27. A reception for former presidents was held at the Campus Center in the forenoon, followed by the noon Alumni Luncheon with comments by Dr. Robert Wagner ('36), interim president in 1971. The evening Alumni Banquet featured a concert by the DWU Highlanders and a keynote speech by President James Beddow. This was followed by a Centennial Ball at the Corn Palace, hosted by Dr. and Mrs. Beddow.

The First United Methodist Church hosted the Centennial Worship Service on Sunday morning, April 28. President Beddow presented the sermon. Worship music was brought by the combined DWU Concert Choir and the First United Methodist Senior Choir. The week's activities were concluded with an Honors Convocation program on Sunday afternoon.

Baccalaureate services were held in the First United Methodist Church on May 12, 1985 with Dr. Donald Veglahn, Superintendent of the Southern District, as speaker. Commencement followed that afternoon, with an address by Bishop Edwin C. Boulton. A presentation of Egil Hovland's "Saul" by Dakota Wesleyan University students and faculty concluded the Centennial celebrations.

Born of a denomination's concern for the propagation of its faith and a frontier town's eagerness for growth, Dakota Wesleyan University has served both well. The college has provided a training ground for hundreds of young men and women who have entered Christian vocations, including missionaries, church workers, bishops, seminary presidents, and YMCA executives. On any given Sunday its alumni fill a large portion of the Methodist pulpits in South Dakota. The church, in turn, has maintained its support through local congregations, the Dakota Conference, and the Board of Education of the General Conference of the Methodist Church. Wesleyan's claim to being a church school is not based on a tenuous historic fact, but on a vital relationship which greatly benefits both institutions.

A close tie also exists between Dakota Wesleyan University and its parent town, Mitchell. The city was instrumental in having the college located at its present site. It provided assistance in the dark days following the fire of 1888, helped to raise funds for the construction of the new College Hall, and has been the school's benefactor in countless other ways. Many of its businessmen and professional people, both Methodists and non-Methodists, have served with singular loyalty as officers of the Board of Trustees. In return, Wesleyan has served as a community college, with as high as one-third of the student body drawn from the local area. It has also been a major business asset and a cultural center for the town. The accolade, "Dakota Wesleyan University, Pride of the Prairie," is well merited.

Endnotes

Chapter I:

1 Septimus W. Ingham, "History of Dakota Mission — First Year, 1860-1861" (Unpublished manuscript in the Archives of the United Methodist Church, Dakota Conference, Mitchell, SD), unpaginated.

2 Gary T. Notson, "Methodist Episcopal Church," Doane Robinson, *A History of South Dakota* (3 vols., Chicago & New York, 1930), I, pp. 454-456; Walter B. Heyler, *The Rise of the Methodist Episcopal Church in South Dakota, from the beginning to the year 1885* (unpublished M.A. thesis, Northwestern University, 1923), pp. 64-84.

3 Martin Osterhaus, Comments at the celebration of the seventy-fifth anniversary of the First Methodist Church, Mitchell, SD, February 14, 1959.

4 *Seventy-Five Years of Mitchell Methodism*, a booklet prepared for the seventy-fifth anniversary of the First Methodist Church (Mitchell, SD, 1958), pp. 4, 5.

5 George P. Schmidt, *The Liberal Arts College: A Chapter in American Cultural History* (New Jersey, 1957), p. 31.

6 Sara Squire Tipple (ed.), *The Heart of Asbury's Journal* (New York, 1904), 405; Halford E. Luccock and Paul Hutchinson, *The Story of Methodism* (New York, 1926), p. 57.

7 Schmidt, *The Liberal Arts College*, p. 32.

8 Frederick Rudolph, *The American College and University, a history* (New York, 1962), p. 57.

9 Luccock, *The Story of Methodism*, p. 360.

10 Dakota Mission Conference of the Methodist Episcopal Church, *Minutes of the First Session*, 1880, p. 2. Hereafter referred to as Dakota Mission, *Minutes*, with appropriate year.

11 The Secretary of State has no record of the incorporation of Dakota University and College Alliance (personal letter from Miss Alma Larson, Secretary of State, to the author, dated February 9, 1970). It is, however, verified by Robinson, *History of South Dakota*, V. I, p. 443; by church and school historians who had access to early records; and by legal documents.

12 Wilmot Whitfield, Yankton, D.T.; Robert C. Glass, Algona, Iowa; M. McKendree Tooke, Rockford, Illinois; and Ira N. Pardee, Sioux City, Iowa. These also served as a temporary Board of Directors and officers. *Articles of Incorporation of Dakota University and College Alliance*, 1883.

13 Dakota Mission, *Minutes*, 1883, p. 36. The offers were as follows: Ordway — an undivided half of 600 acres of land, 80 acres for campus, 50 town lots; 240 acres seven miles from village; $50,000 to erect first building, and a cabinet of Natural History valued at $10,000. Mitchell — 640 acres of land within city limits; 640 acres adjoining city limits; $60,000 in donations and sub-

109

scriptions, and two tracts of land to be sold for endowment fund. Huron — 200 acres of land; $20,000, and a residence for the President of the institution.

[14] *Mitchell Capital* (Mitchell, South Dakota), April 4,1884; April 18, 1884; May 2, 1884: "Statement of Facts," *Dakota University and College Alliance vs. Dakota University, Amanda M. Bowdle and Ralph Bowdle*, Circuit Court, Davison County, South Dakota, April 1, 1904.

[15] Dakota Mission, *Minutes*, 1884, p. 57.

[16] O. W. Coursey, *A History of Dakota Wesleyan University for Fifty Years, 1885-1935* (Mitchell, South Dakota, 1935), pp. 23, 24.

[17] Dakota Mission, *Minutes*, 1884, pp. 69-70.

[18] *Mitchell Capital*, February 6 and 13, 1885.

[19] Dakota University was incorporated April 27, 1885, by Ira N. Pardee, Wilmot Whitfield, M. McKendree Tooke, William Brush, Lewis Hartsough, A. W. Hager, E. S. Ormsby, O. S. Basford and Hiram Barber, Jr. The first three were also among those who had filed the 1883 corporation. *Articles of Incorporation of Dakota University*, 1885, Mitchell, South Dakota.

[20] Dakota Conference of the Methodist Episcopal Church, *Minutes of the First Annual Session*, 1885, p. 98. Hereafter referred to as Dakota Conference, *Minutes*, with appropriate year.

[21] Dakota Conference, *Minutes*, 1885, pp. 95, 96.

[22] *Ibid.*, 1886, pp. 108, 118.

Chapter II:

[1] *First Biennial Catalogue of Dakota University*, 1885-1887, p. 35. The catalogs of Dakota Wesleyan University are published under a variety of titles. They will hereafter be cited as *Catalog*, with appropriate year.

[2] Commonly referred to as red granite. The quartzite for Merrill Memorial Hall was quarried at Sioux Falls, South Dakota.

[3] Schmidt, *The Liberal Arts College*, p. 104.

[4] Heyler, *The Rise of the Methodist Episcopal Church in South Dakota*, p. 80; Arthur C. Shepherd, "Historical Sketch of Dakota Wesleyan University," IX, p. 8. Hereafter referred to as Shepherd, "Historical Sketch."

[5] *Minutes* of the Board of Directors of Dakota University, quoted in Coursey, *A History of Dakota Wesleyan University*, pp. 51-53.

[6] Dakota Conference, *Minutes*, 1888, p. 172.

[7] Coursey, *A History of Dakota Wesleyan University*, pp. 57-59.

[8] Samuel Eliot Morison, *Three Centuries of Harvard: 1636-1936* (Cambridge, Massachusetts, 1937), p. 46.

[9] Coursey, *A History of Dakota Wesleyan University*, p. 65.

[10] Appendix E.

[11] Rudolph, *The American College and University*, p. 331.

[12] Classical, scientific, normal, preparatory, music, medicine, mechanics, commercial, law, home education, and theology. *Articles of Incorporation of Dakota University*, Article VI.

[13] Appendix E.

[14] Information on course offerings and requirements are taken from the college catalogs unless otherwise stated.

[15] Information on the Normal Department is taken from *Catalogs*, 1885-1903; "A Report on the Teacher Education Program at Dakota Wesleyan University," submitted to the National Council for Accreditation of Teacher Education (mimeograph, Dakota Wesleyan University, Mitchell, South Dakota, 1969), pp. 1-2; Halvin S. Johnson, *A History of the Department of Education of Dakota Wesleyan University* (unpublished M.A. thesis, University of South Dakota), pp. 12-24.

[16] The college catalog of 1894 makes mention of cooperation with a [Methodist] federation of colleges, a phrase used in early presentations of the University Senate plan. The Board of Education of the United Methodist Church has no systematic record of when colleges were first placed on the approved list. (Letter from Revayne Stewart, secretary to Dr. R. N. Bender of the Board of Education, addressed to the author, dated February 19, 1970).

[17] Myron F. Wicke, *A Brief History of the University Senate of the Methodist Church* (Nashville, Tennessee, 1956), pp. 6-11.

[18] Dr. Twilley, professor of natural science, 1895-96.

[19] Ethan T. Colton, Sr., *Memoirs of Ethan T. Colton, Sr. 1872-1952*, rev. 1968. (Mimeograph, Archives of the United Methodist Church, Dakota Conference, Mitchell, South Dakota), p. 21. Hereafter cited as Colton, *Memoirs*.

[20] *Phreno Cosmian*, June 1894. The *Phreno Cosmian* is the student newspaper at Dakota Wesleyan University.

[21] A. C. Shepherd, "Reminiscences of Life at Dakota University in the Early Days", *Phreno Cosmian*, May 1900.

[22] Gustavus Loevenger, letter to the alumni editor, *Phreno Cosmian*, December 1904, pp. 18-19.

[23] Ethan T. Colton, Sr., letter addressed to the author, dated December 31, 1969.

[24] Madge Corwin Chapman, Letter to Judge Mallory, to be read to the fiftieth anniversary of her class, May 29, 1952, in Mitchell. Dated May 22, 1952 (Alumni Case, Layne Library, Dakota Wesleyan University, Mitchell, South Dakota). Hereafter cited as Chapman, Letter.

[25] *Ibid.*

[26] James McLaird, "Of Preachers, Poets, and Pines: Badger Clark writes to Ralph Shearer, 1929-1949," *South Dakota History*, Winter 1983, p. 355.

111

[27] *Phreno Cosmian*, November 13, 1945, "Bobbs' Reminisce."

[28] Colton, *Memoirs*, p. 18.

[29] *Ibid.*, p. 23.

[30] J P Hauser, "Report of the President, May 28, 1897, March 24, 1898", *Statistical Record of the Y.M.C.A.* (located in basement vault, Dakota Wesleyan University), unpaginated; Colton, *Memoirs*, pp. 21, 27-84; Nellie M. Barker, letter addressed to Miss Carhart, printed in the *Phreno Cosmian*, January 1905.

[31] *Phreno Cosmian*, May 1903.

[32] Colton, *Memoirs*, p. 18.

[33] *Ibid.*, pp. 18-19.

[34] *Phreno Cosmian*, May 1903.

[35] Colton, *Memoirs*, p. 18.

[36] *D.W.U., Old Items*, "Faculty Minutes," November 22, 1901 (unpublished collection at Dakota Wesleyan University, Mitchell, South Dakota), p. 201.

[37] J. Leonard Jennewein, "Dakota Methodism and Higher Education," Matthew D. Smith (ed.), *Circuit Riders of the Middle Border* (1965), p. 110. Hereafter cited as Jennewein, "Dakota Methodism and Higher Education."

[38] Coursey, *A History of Dakota Wesleyan University*, p. 151.

[39] "A Report on the Teacher Education Program at Dakota Wesleyan University," p. 1.

[40] Dakota Conference, *Minutes*, 1886, "Report of the Committee on Education", p. 118.

[41] A. Duncan, "History," *Tumbleweed*, 1901, pp. 15-16.

[42] Dakota Conference, *Minutes*, 1888, "Report of the Committee on Education", p. 190; 1889, "Report of the Board of Directors", p. 224.

[43] *Ibid.*, 1896, "Report of the Committee on Education," pp. 28-30.

[44] Jennewein, "Dakota Methodism and Higher Education," p. 112.

Chapter III:

[1] "Amendments to Articles of Incorporation of the Dakota University," dated June 14-15, 1904, filed November 12, 1904, *D.W.U. Papers* (Archives of the United Methodist Church, Dakota Conference, Mitchell, South Dakota). The official change in name is confirmed by the Secretary of State.

[2] Dakota Conference, *Minutes*, 1905, pp. 37, 41.

[3] Harry H. Woodward, *A History of Black Hills College* (unpublished M.A. thesis, University of South Dakota, 1931).

[4] *Phreno Cosmian*, March 4, 1915, "Professor Stout Reviews Institution's Growth."

[5] "By-laws of the Board of Directors of Dakota Wesleyan University," Article I, Section 4, as recorded in Board of Directors of Dakota Wesleyan University, *Minutes* (unpublished manuscript in the Business Office, Dakota Wesleyan University, Mitchell, South Dakota), June 1, 1915, p. 218. Hereafter referred to as Board, *Minutes*, with appropriate date.

[6] Board, *Minutes*, March 27, 1914, "Report of the President," p. 190; June 9, 1914, pp. 201-202; *Phreno Cosmian*, May 28, 1914.

[7] Board, *Minutes*, June 6, 1916, "Report of the President," pp. 252-256; "W" Scrapbooks (Alumni Case, Layne Library, Dakota Wesleyan University, Mitchell, South Dakota).

[8] Board, *Minutes*, May 10, 1916, p. 266.

[9] Board, *Minutes*, "Report of the President," June 8, 1920, p. 384.

[10] Board, *Minutes*, December 21, 1925, pp. 650-51.

[11] *Ibid.*, May 31, 1926, p. 664.

[12] Richard Hofstadter and C. Dewitt Hardy, *The Development and Scope of Higher Education in the United States* (New York, 1952), p. 48.

[13] Letter from Joseph J. Semrow, associate executive secretary of the North Central Association of Colleges and Secondary Schools, addressed to the author, December 12, 1969.

[14] *Phreno Cosmian*, March 23, 1926.

[15] Vernon van Patter, Master of Commercial Science, conferred June 2, 1915. Thesis: *Some General Social Observations on Rural Life, together with a Social Study of a Northern Minnesota Township, and the Socializing Efforts of the Township's Consolidated Rural Schools* (located in Alumni Case, Layne Library, Dakota Wesleyan University, Mitchell, South Dakota).

[16] Information on a teacher training program was taken from the college *Catalogs*; Johnson, *A History of the Department of Education at Dakota Wesleyan University*, pp. 23-31; "A Report on the Teacher Education Program at Dakota Wesleyan University." Submitted to the National Council for the Accreditation of Teacher Education. Mimeograph, Mitchell, South Dakota, 1969.

[17] Leona Lloyd Burr, *Dear Ones at Home, Autobiography*. Stickney, South Dakota; Argus Printers, 1965.

[18] Information on boarding clubs was obtained by personal interviews with Matthew D. Smith, November 12, 1969, and William Kaye, November 28, 1969.

[19] Excerpt from the unpublished memoirs of Matthew D. Smith, entitled *Educational Ventures Under Five Flags*, Dakota Wesleyan University, *Bulletin*, V. 62, September 1968, pp. 6-7.

[20] *Ibid.*, pp. 37-39.

[21] Board, *Minutes*, May 31, 1928, p. 781.

[22] *Phreno Cosmian*, "Campus Forum," February 6, 1929.

23 Dakota Wesleyan Forensic Board, *Minutes*, 1916-1924 (manuscript and clippings, Dakota Wesleyan University, Mitchell, South Dakota), p. 82.

24 *Phreno Cosmian*, January 12, 1926.

25 Information on forensics was taken from the *Phreno Cosmian*; Dakota Wesleyan Forensic Board, *Minutes*, 1916-1924; Elmer Knudson, *The History of Speech Education at Dakota Wesleyan University, 1885-1952* (unpublished M.A. thesis, University of South Dakota, 1954); Jerry Tippens, *The Voice of the Tiger, A History of Speech Education at Dakota Wesleyan University Forensics Department*, written in connection with a speech course at Dakota Wesleyan University (unpublished manuscript, Dakota Wesleyan University, Mitchell, South Dakota, 1952).

26 Leona Lloyd Burr, *Dear Ones at Home*, p. 7.

27 Lester Belding, *A History and Survey of Physical Education and Athletics in the South Dakota Intercollegiate Athletic Conference* (Unpublished M.A. thesis, State University of Iowa, 1940), pp. 9-10.

28 *Phreno Cosmian*, November 24, 1925; December 8, 1925.

29 John Prince Jenkins, "Report," Board, *Minutes*, June 5, 1912, pp. 115-116.

30 *Ibid.*, June 9, 1914, p. 197.

Chapter IV:

1 Earl Roadman, quoted by J. Leonard Jennewein in Smith, *Circuit Riders of the Middle Border*, p. 117.

2 Board, *Minutes*, November 15, 1932, pp. 31b-31c.

3 Melvin W. Hyde, "Report," Board, *Minutes*, June 3, 1935, p. 125.

4 Earl Roadman, et. al., "Two and a Half Dozen" (mimeographed manuscript in Alumni Case, Layne Library, Dakota Wesleyan University), p. 44. Hereafter cited as Roadman, "Two and a Half Dozen."

5 Since the By-laws specified that the diplomas had to be signed by the president, Roadman was given a leave of absence without pay from April 15 to June 10, 1936. Sweetland was named acting president and took over the duties of the office on May 9, 1936. Board, *Minutes*, May 9, 1936, pp. 153, 157; June 8, 1936, p. 164.

6 Dakota Conference, *Minutes*, 1936, pp. 60-61; Board, *Minutes*, September 14, 1936, pp. 193-94; *Phreno Cosmian*, October 20, 1936; S. H. Shurtleff, letters to H. B. Tysell, dated October 16, 1936 (folder containing correspondence and other materials relating to Sweetland's administration, Dakota Wesleyan University, Mitchell, South Dakota).

7 *Phreno Cosmian*, May 25, 1936.

[8] Board, *Minutes*, February 16, 1937, p. 210; *Mitchell Gazette*, February 11, 1937.

[9] Board, *Minutes*, May 22, 1937, pp. 211-213; Personal interview with Dr. Frank E. Lockridge, chairman of the investigating committee, January 30, 1970.

[10] A fund-raising program of the General Conference of the Methodist Church which ran from 1944 to 1948 for the strengthening of essential church programs. Myron F. Wicke, *The Methodist Church and Higher Education, 1939-64* (Nashville, Tennessee, 1965), p. 19. Crusade for Christ funds allotted to Dakota Wesleyan were raised within the Dakota Conference.

[11] *Dakota Wesleyan University Bulletin*, XVI, January 1942.

[12] Board, *Minutes*, May 26, 1947, pp. 554-56.

[13] Jennewein, "Dakota Methodism and Higher Education," *Circuit Riders of the Middle Border*, pp. 118-119.

[14] Board, *Minutes*, "University Senate Report on Dakota Wesleyan University," January 8, 1951; Board, *Minutes*, May 28, 1951, unpaginated.

[15] *Catalog*, 1950-51, pp. 44, 76-77.

[16] Johnson, *History of Teacher Education at Dakota Wesleyan University*, pp. 46-48.

[17] *Ibid.*, pp. 39-40.

[18] Katherine Tracy Schilling, *The History of Dramatic Art at Dakota Wesleyan University, 1885-1986*. Unpublished M.A. thesis, University of South Dakota, 1957, pp. 51-89.

[19] Personal interview with Loretta Smith.

[20] Elmer Knudson, *The History of Speech Education at Dakota Wesleyan University, 1885-1952* (Unpublished M.A. thesis, University of South Dakota, 1954), pp. 62-64; Tippens, *The Voice of the Tiger*, pp. 5-6, 10-11; *Tumbleweed*, 1940, pp. 35-36; *Phreno Cosmian*, May 31, 1935, February 9, 1943, September 16, 1955.

[21] Ernest A. Carhart, Alumni Questionnaire, 1983.

[22] Personal interview with Edna Blessing Leach, January 30, 1970.

[23] Roadman, "Two and a Half Dozen," p. 48.

[24] "D.W.U. History," a skit prepared for an assembly program by the library staff and the Writer's Club, March 20, 1959 (Alumni file, Layne Library, Dakota Wesleyan University), p. 11.

[25] Ethel Johnson Hughes, Alumni Questionnaire, 1983.

[26] Belding, *A History and Survey of Physical Education and Athletics*, pp. 10-11, 146; Belding, letter to the editor, *Phreno Cosmian*, February 14, 1939.

[27] Personal interview with Donald Screes, Director of Alumni Affairs, Dakota Wesleyan University, December 11, 1992.

[28] Personal interview with Gordon Fosness, February 27, 1970.

Chapter V:

[1] Smith, *Ventures in Christian Education*, p. 51.

[2] *Ibid.*, pp. 151-152. Gordon Rollins, letter to author, January 3, 1993. Hereafter cited as Rollins, letter, with date.

[3] Board, *Minutes*, May 15, 1954.

[4] Rollins, letter, January 5, 1993.

[5] *Ibid.*, January 3, 1993.

[6] Leland D. Case (comp.), *Thirty Years of FMB, 1939-1969.* Papers documenting the origin and growth of the Friends of the Middle Border, Dakota Wesleyan University, Mitchell, South Dakota; unpaginated. Class in Spoken Communication 103, written accounts of the fire (manuscripts, Dakota Wesleyan University); faculty reminiscences of the fire (manuscripts, Dakota Wesleyan University), February 24, 1958.

[7] Rollins, letter, January 3, 1993.

[8] Matthew D. Smith, student chapel address, quoted in *Dakota Wesleyan University Bulletin*, V. 50, January 1956.

[9] *Dakota Wesleyan University Bulletin*, V. 52, 1958.

[10] Financial information from Gordon Rollins.

[11] Board, *Minutes*, "Minutes of the Executive Committee," February 25, 1971.

[12] *Dakota Wesleyan University Bulletin*, V. 54, 1960.

[13] "Special Report;" Statements made at a confidential session held in Graham Hall at Dakota Wesleyan University on Tuesday, January 24, 1961. Listening to the eight students present were Jerry Baysore, Emery Bogle, Donald Messer, and Mr. Leonard Jennewein.

[14] Donald Messer, "Excellence: THE HUMAN FACTOR." Address at 100th Anniversary Banquet, Dakota Wesleyan University, Mitchell, SD, April 26, 1985.

[15] Johnson, *History of Teacher Education at Dakota Wesleyan University*, pp. 39, 40.

[16] Schilling, *A History of Dramatic Art at Dakota Wesleyan University*, pp. 51-89; *Catalogs, Phreno Cosmians, passim.*

[17] Quote is taken from Deed of Gift, dated July 2, 1962.

[18] Knudson, *The History of Speech Education at Dakota Wesleyan University*, pp. 62-64; Tippens, *The Voice of the Tiger*, pp. 5-6, 10-11; *Phreno Cosmian*, September 16, 1955.

[19] *Tumbleweed*, 1959, p. 66.

[20] *Ibid.*, 1959, *Passim*; *Catalog* 1958-60, pp. 11-13.

[21] Orlando J. Goering, McLaird & Coates; "The Candy Controversy: A Study in Community Censorship," (unpublished manuscript), 1970.

22 Figures from the Registrar's office.

23 *Tumbleweed*, 1966, p. 118.

24 Appendix D: FINANCIAL OVERVIEW.

Chapter VI:

1 James Beddow, "College of the Prairie: Dakota Wesleyan University," *From Idea to Institution: HIGHER EDUCATION IN SOUTH DAKOTA*, Herbert T. Hoover, et.al., editor. University of South Dakota Press, Vermillion, 1989, p. 190. Hereafter cited as Beddow, "College of the Prairie."

2 Donald E. Messer, "Reflections on My DWU Presidency," July 1992. Unpublished manuscript, pp. 1-2. Hereafter cited as Messer, "Reflections."

3 Board, *Minutes*, "Report of Cummerford Corporation Financial Survey," by Frank H. Hanover. Feb. 19, 1971, p. 2.

4 Board, *Minutes*, Feb. 19, 1971, pp. 2-3.

5 *Ibid.* "Minutes of the Executive Committee Meeting," Feb. 25, 1971.

6 *Ibid.* "Minutes of the Executive Committee Meeting," May 14, 1971; "Report of the Interim President," May 19, 1971.

7 "The Greene Report," Edward E. Greene, Director of Finance and Planning, Wofford College, South Carolina.

8 Messer, "Reflections", p. 3.

9 Beddow, "College of the Prairie," p. 190.

10 Donald E. Messer, "A Vision for the 1980's and Beyond." Mimeographed manuscript. Hereafter cited as Messer, "A Vision."

11 *Ibid.*, p. 10.

12 Messer, "Reflections," pp. 6-8.

13 *Ibid.*, p. 8.

14 Board, *Minutes*, "The President's Report," May 21, 1977.

15 Dr. Gold Hauser was the first white child born in the Black Hills and a lifelong missionary.

16 Board, *Minutes*, "Report of the Executive Committee," July 17, 1970.

17 *Faculty Minutes*, October 28, 1983.

18 Messer, "Reflections," pp.8-9.

19 *Phreno Cosmian*, Vol. 96, Feb. 25, 1983.

20 Survey, Methodist Quadrennial Program for Aid to Higher Education; Board of Education of the United Methodist Church, 1956-1960.

117

[21] Board, *Minutes*, Oct. 28, 1983. "Directions of Student Affairs at DWU," by President James Beddow. Presented at the fall faculty workshop.

[22] Faculty, *Minutes*, Aug. 30-31, 1984; Sept. 19, 1984.

[23] James Beddow, "Institutional Journey," 1984.

[24] *Phreno Cosmian*, Feb. 3, 1984.

[25] *Tumbleweed*, 1985.

[26] Board, *Minutes*, Religious Life Program Review Update for Trustees. April 26, 1985.

[27] *Tumbleweed*, 1985.

APPENDIX A

Dakota Wesleyan University Leadership

Presidents

William Brush	1885-1891	Leon C. Sweetland	1936-1937
Charles O. Merica	1891-1892	Joseph H. Edge	1937-1946
William Graham	1893-1903	Samuel Hilburn	1946-1951
Thomas Nicholson	1903-1908	Matthew D. Smith	1952-1958
Samuel L. Kerfoot	1908-1912	Jack J. Early	1958-1969
William G. Seaman	1912-1916	Robert R. Huddleston	1969-1971
W.D. Schermerhorn	1917-1922	Robert H. Wagner (interim)	1971
Edward D. Kohlstedt	1922-1927	Donald E. Messer	1971-1981
Earl A. Roadman	1927-1936	James B. Beddow	1981-1994

Board of Trustees

In 1985, the Board of Trustees consisted of thirty-six voting members and four ex-officio members, namely the Bishop of the Dakotas Area of the United Methodist Church and the three district superintendents of the South Dakota Conference of the United Methodist Church. Six of the members were nominated by the Conference Council on Ministries. The Board has a pattern of shared leadership with faculty and students. The first Board of Directors, as listed in the 1883 Articles of Incorporation, consisted of Wilmot Whitfield, president; Robert C. Glass, vice president; M. McKendree Tooke, secretary; and Ira N. Pardee, treasurer. According to the records available, the following have served as chair of the Board since 1885:

Ira N. Pardee	May 1885-Jan. 1887	S. E. Morris	1910-1924
Bishop Thomas Bowman		B. A. Bobb	1924-1937
	Jan.-June 1887	Lauritz Miller	1937-1942
A. J. Edgerton	1887-1888	A. F. Test	1942-1943
T. E. Blanchard	1888-1893	B. A. Bobb	1943-1945
E. B. Bracy	1894-1895	Bradley Young	1945-1958
T. E. Blanchard	1895-1896	Steve Ptak	1958-1969
E. B. Bracy	1897-1898	Boyd Knox	1969-1981
J. O. Dobson	1898-1899	Don Swanson	1981-1984
I. W. Seaman	1899-1910	Richard Cutler	1984-1985

APPENDIX B

Academic Deans of Dakota Wesleyan University

Samuel Weir	1911-1913	Marcus A. Chase	1947-1951
Clarence V. Gilliland	1913-1919	Jesse J. Knox	1951-1956
Merrill Jacob Holmes	1919-1926	Thomas D. Henson	1956-1972
Earl Kansas Hildbrand	1926-1929	Maynard Cochrane	1972-1975
Chester L. Rich	1929-1934	John Hartung	1975-1978
Melvin W. Hyde	1934-1936	Jerry Trimble	1978-1979
Matthew D. Smith	1936-1944	Helen Trimble	1979-
Earle E. Emme	1944-1947		

APPENDIX C

Business Managers of Dakota Wesleyan University

The term "business manager" first appears in 1907. Prior to that time the designation "finance secretary" was used. Records for the early years are incomplete. Current and endowment funds were separated in 1916. Those listed were in charge of the current fund. Beginning with John F. Way, the business manager of the college also served as the treasurer of the Board of Directors.

T. A. Duncan	1887-1900	Raymond H. Gregg	1930-1932
(listed intermittently)		Harmon W. Brown	1932-1946
W. I. Graham	1903	Gordon S. Rollins	1946-1975
Lachen Maclean	1906	Dennis Bolen	1975-1982
Joseph Graham	1907-1909	Michael Ewald	1982-1983
Harry Havens	1909-1910	Richard Wahlstrom	1983-
John Foote Way	1910-1930		

APPENDIX D

Financial Overview

Fiscal Year	Current Fund Operating Budget*	Tuition Only	Endowment Fund	Gift Annuities	Buildings and Grounds
1910	$61,675	$30	$97,049	$0	$236,505
1920	149,801	100	336,184	0	340,259
1930	94,986	150	563,275	23,100	536,131
1940	140,939	150	595,723	7,500	553,795
1950	292,348	300	554,414	27,719	577,568
1960	487,537	350	992,291	42,715	1,338,801
1970	1,532,724	875	1,254,933	183,834	4,118,210
1980	2,226,567	2,065	2,704,409	713,427	4,574,315
1981	2,509,753	2,315	2,751,029	830,419	4,665,224
1982	2,649,266	3,065	2,967,064	815,710	4,880,470
1983	3,329,339	3,280	3,149,262	769,515	4,908,782
1984	3,352,733	3,512	3,763,832	815,136	5,129,440
1985	4,210,260	3,870	3,907,814	812,177	6,432,239

* Including auxiliary enterprises.

APPENDIX E

Table 1: Enrollment, 1885-1903

Year	Regular Departments			Special Departments			Elocution	Net Total
	College	Preparatory*	Normal	Commercial**	Music	Art		
1885-87	4	85	—	27	14	8	—	106
1887-89	12	40	64	75	11	7	15	185
1889-91	—	106	38	24	61	14	16	224
1892	17	101	53	56	49	22	42	254
1893	6	77	71	52	45	—	99	255
1893-95	28	116	57	62	79	47	114	309
1895-97	44	130	52	43	85	—	94	226
1898	49	99	60	44	42	30	—	264
1899	41	158	65	51	53	32	—	328
1900	49	228	73	51	71	27	—	358
1901	68	150	49	48	79	40	75	365
1902	50	161	70	65	70	34	22	336
1903	71	186	79	56	88	30	31	400

*Preparatory figures include subpreparatory and special students.
**Commercial figures include stenography and typewriting students.
Source: College catalogs.

Table 2: Enrollment, 1903-1930

Year	College of L.A.	Academy	Normal	Music	Commercial	Art	Elocution	Net Total	Summer
1903-04								400	—
1904-05	55	148	37	85	43	50	20	345	—
1905-06	59	144	83	120	111	57	21	463	—
1906-07	79	186	77	197	177	46	53	526	121
1907-08	113	167	107	200	129	47	74		143
1908-09	145	112	59	197	105	40	50	543	96
1909-10	122	118	54	227	143	31	63	568	96
1910-11	106	119	54	177	140	53	66	548	165
1911-12	147	80	38	160	106	29	64	429	145
1912-13	133	63	72	134	124	40	58	407	187
1913-14	114	60	62	230	152	37	—	430	84
1914-15	197	117	—	100	—	30	—	363	156
1915-16	213	111	—	98	—	28	—	369	119
1916-17	183	83	—	78	—	—	—	301	136
1917-18	179	94	—	74	—	—	—	303	98
1918-19	253	161	—	204	—	—	—	534	235
1919-20	268	177	—	196	—	—	—	526	182
1920-21	293	115	—	115	—	—	—	450	215
1921-22				(no records available)					
1922-23	320	59	—	116	—	—	—	431	233
1923-24	329	45	—	106	—	—	—	394	230
1924-25	343	35	—	51	—	—	—	399	219
1925-26	349	66	—	24	—	—	—	397	188
1926-27	335	—	—	45	—	—	—	356	148
1927-28	307	—	—	83	—	—	—	332	111
1928-29	343	—	—	100	—	—	—	384	126
1929-30	327	—	—	110	—	—	—	366	82

Source: College catalogs.

Table 3: Enrollment, 1930-1960

Year	College Full-time	Miscellaneous (non-credit, student nurses, etc.)	Music	College-Grand Total	Summer School	Net Total* Plus Summer School
1930-31	362	—	167	529	168	570
1931-32	352	—	292	644	169	654
1932-33	333	—	215	548	162	544
1933-34	312	—	163	475	104	461
1934-35	361	33	150	544	163	473
1935-36	350	17	130	497	138	479
1936-37	396	44	88	528	155	523
1937-38	344	43	65	552	150	433
1938-39	375	15	45	435	106	454
1939-40	366	26	41	427	126	470
1940-41	328	28	39	395	138	411
1941-42	283	44	34	361	75	347
1942-43	256	12	28	306	124	346
1943-44			(no records available)			
1944-45	144	16	6	166	121	267
1945-46	238	19	9	256	98	337
1946-47	440	45	26	511	102	518
1947-48	445	29	27	501	131	530
1948-49	402	—	62	464	127	514
1949-50	328	—	45	373	214	454
1950-51			(no records available)			
1951-52	190	51	—	241	105	306
1952-53	316	—	79	395	94	410
1953-54	353	—	45	398	111	469
1954-55	274	119	16	409	154	511
1955-56	328	122	20	470	160	570
1956-57	354	139	41	534	179	644
1957-58	369	112	44	525	185	630
1958-59	391	—	—	**448	243	**679
1959-60	370	—	—	**425	266	**623

Source: 1930-1958, college catalogs; 1958-1960, record in the Registrar's office.

*Net total equals grand total (all students, full-time and part-time) for nine months minus repeated names.

**Totals for these two years are based on full-time students plus part-time equated to full-time (two half-time students equal one full-time load). This is a more accurate representation of actual enrollment. For example, the last column for 1957-1958 reads 630 when all names are counted but only 541 when part-time enrollment is equated to full-time. Similar figures for preceding years were not available in the Registrar's office.

Table 4: Enrollment, 1960-1985

	SUMMER	FALL		SPRING	
		FT	PT	FT	PT
1960	266	503	99		
1961	353	606	103	466	256
1962	295	542	72	522	96
1963	346	537	100	506	93
1964	361	560	78	512	61
1965	411	616	125	545	68
1966	420	712	138	592	86
1967	396	711	107	678	85
1968	401	714	103	671	116
1969	350	613	149	667	135
1970	289	519	94	556	144
1971	305	490	83	470	93
1972	184	405	88	426	86
1973	227	384	82	392	117
1974	209	408	73	352	75
1975	221	470	69	405	93
1976	233	454	120	442	78
1977	236	485	106	427	153
1978	246	444	72	448	104
1979	317	468	61	406	100
1980	275			434	44
1981	247	450	96	446	121
1982	319	415	96	424	108
1983	305	391	104	400	145
1984	344	474	97	375	118
1985	327	581	111	467	121

APPENDIX F

Table 1: Graduates, 1885-1903

Year	College	Normal	Music	Art
1887-88	1	3	—	—
1888-89	3	3	—	—
1889-90	—	—	—	—
1890-91	—	3	—	—
1891-81	3	5	1	—
1892-93	—	3	—	—
1893-94	—	4	—	—
1894-95	—	4	2	—
1895-96	—	5	3	—
1896-97	7	7	2	—
1897-98	5	18	—	—
1898-99	6	21	1	—
1899-1900	4	15	1	1
1900-01	3	11	3	1
1901-02	7	15	1	1
1902-03	6	12	4	2
TOTALS	45	129	18	4

Source: *Dakota University Bulletin*, II (April-June 1904), pp. 88-89.

Table 2: Graduate Degrees and Most Frequently Chosen Majors

Year	Bachelor		A.A.		2 yr. Ed. Mus. Ed.	UHS Academy
1918	22		—		11	12
1926	47		—		32	9
	History	12				
	Education	9				
	Economics	7				
1935	50		—		39	—
	History	7				
	English	6				
	Education	6				
1945	15		—		19	—
	Economics	3				
1955	38		—		19	—
	Bus. Adm.	6				
	Soc. Sci.	5				
1965	180		—		1	—
	Education	28				
	History	24				
	Math	19				
	Sociology	16				
	Bus. Adm.	15				
	English	14				
1975	121		48		—	—
	Psychology	18	Nursing	38		
	Biology	17	MLT*	10		
	Bus. Adm.	16				
	Education	10				
1983	122		56		—	—
	Bus. Adm.	29	Nursing	36		
	Psychology	16				
	H/PER*	16				
1984	67		68		—	—
			Nursing	65		
1985	48		77		—	—
	Bus. Adm.	21	Nursing	68		
	Psychology	9	Bus. Adm.	9		

*MLT=Medical Licensed Technician; H/PER=Health, Physical Ed., Recreation.
Information taken from college catalogs.

APPENDIX G

Major Benefactors

Dakota Wesleyan University has enjoyed the monetary support of a wide constituency. A total of 2,610 donors of gifts ranging from one dollar to over one million dollars is listed in the Agenda for Excellence Report on the first century's last campaign (1983-1986). The following is a partial list of major benefactors from 1885 to 1986 and includes donors of $15,000 or more for the Agenda for Excellence campaign.

Mrs. Earline Roadman
Mr. & Mrs. Harland H. Allen
Mr. & Mrs. Herman Assmus
Dr. & James Beddow
Dr. & Mrs. John Billion
Mr. & Mrs. Oscar C. Blaine
Mr. & Mrs. Melvin Blessing
Dr. B. A. Bobb
Belle Butterfield
Dr. & Mrs. Paul R. Christen*
Mr. & Mrs. Philip C. Christen
Mr. & Mrs. Arthur S. Cory
Mr. & Mrs. Richard Cutler
Grace Bliss Dayton
Dr. Charles S. Dewey
Mr. & Mrs. Cecil W. Duncan
Lucille J. Edmonds
Gladys L. Ehrstrom
Mr. & Mrs. David G. Elhoff
Mr. & Mrs. Ray Eppel
Dr. Garold Faber
Mr. & Mrs. Vern A. Fairfield
Mr. & Mrs. Arthur Fishbeck
Mr. Howard D. Giese
Mr. & Mrs. Paul C. Green
Mrs. Mayme Green
Mr. & Mrs. Owen Garnos
Mr. James S. Hill

Elizabeth Smith Hull
Mr. & Mrs. David R. Jackson
Mr. D. F. Jones
Mr. & Mrs. Rollie R. Kelley
Dr. & Mrs. Boyd Knox
Mahlon & Lawrence Layne
Mr. Philip G. Laurson**
Dr. & Mrs. John Leach
Mrs. Myrtle Tipton Miller
Mrs. Ethel Metzger
Mr. & Mrs. Wallace S. Moore
Joseph & Florence Morrow
Dorothy L. Nelson
Dr. & Mrs. Perry S. Nelson
Henry & Anna Pfeiffer
Mr. & Mrs. Steve Ptak
Dr. & Mrs. Joe Robbie
Mr. & Mrs. Gordon Rollins
Dr. & Mrs. Theodore Roman
Mr. & Mrs. Victor M. Rubert
Mr. & Mrs. Wayne I. Saterlie
Mr. & Mrs. Fred R. Scallin
Dr. & Mrs. Kenneth E. Sherman*
Dr. & Mrs. B. R. Skogmo
Mr. & Mrs. Glenn A. Soladay
Senator Leland Stanford (CA)
Dr. & Mrs. Franklin C. Stark
Dr. & Mrs. Donald H. Swanson

Mr. & Mrs. Sherman Hill
Mr. & Mrs. Underwood Hilton
Mr. Herbert Hitchcock
Mr. Joseph Hofrichter, III
Mr. & Mrs. Sidney L. Horman
Mr. Frank Howdle
Mrs. Vivienne J. Huber
Mr. George Fredericks
Board of Education, United
 Methodist Church
Burlington Northern Foundation
Bush Foundation
Charles A. Frueauff Foundation
Commercial Trust & Savings Bank
D & E Vending
Ford Foundation
Kresge Foundation
Layne Foundation
Livestock State Bank
National Endowment for the Humanities
Northwest Area Foundation

Alice Parker Trimble
Georgena Smith Tyler
Mr. & Mrs. E. J. Van Westen
Mrs. Dorothy Von Tobel
Ruth & Leone Wagner
Mrs. Glennie M. Whites
Mr. & Mrs. Perry Van Wie
Mr. & Mrs. Erlow Wiseman
Northwestern Bell Telephone Co.
Northwestern Public Service Co.
Norwest Foundation
Randall Stores, Inc.
Rockefeller Board
Sheesley Plumbing & Heating
S. D. Annual Conference, United
 Methodist Church
S. D. Foundation of Private
 Colleges
S. D. United Methodist Foundation
Tessier Sheet Metal Works
Worthington United Methodist
 Church

*Two families have given gifts totaling over one million dollars, namely Dr. & Mrs. Kenneth E. Sherman and Dr. & Mrs. Paul R. Christen.

**The largest single gift prior to the Agenda For Excellence Campaign was the half-million dollar estate of Philip G. Laurson ('07), a former Yale professor.

APPENDIX H

Distinguished Alumni

Alumnus of the Year

To an alumnus who has rendered notable service to his/her profession and society.

Past Recipients:

1958	Frank S. Beck '12
1959	Lawrence Todmen '12
1960	—
1961	Ethan T. Colton '98
1962	Leland D. Case ex'22
1963	Clinton Anderson ex'17
1964	Everett W. Palmer '32
1965	Kenneth M. Harkness '20
1966	Franklin C. Stark '37
1967	Ronald E. Hull '52
1968	Arnold Herbst '42
1969	Elsie Wolcott Hayden '21
1970	Sidney L. Horman '33
1971	George McGovern '46
1972	Melvin W. Hyde '26
1973	Harvey Sander '44
1974	Arthur Raymond '51
1975	Theodore Roman '56
1976	Kenneth Ottis '42
1977	Bill Marutani '50
1978	Richard Schermerhorn '24
1979	Jerry Tippens '52
1980	Marvin Fuller '46
1981	Laurel Archer Copp '56
1982	Robert Steadman '23
1983	—
1984	Larry Bohning '65
1985	Amber Van Burnham '35

Distinguished Alumni

Young Alumnus of the Year

To an alumnus under the age of 35 who has rendered notable service to his/her profession and society.

Past Recipients:

1974 Chris Cain (Bruce Doggett) '65
1975 David Horton '64
1976 David Putman '62
1977 Darrel Leach '63
1978 Don '66 & Evalyn Sougstad Durfee '65
1979 Robert Ohlen '65
1980 Bill Farris '69
1981 Michael Denney '69
1982 George Bittner '71
1983 David Elhoff '72
1984 Douglas Kirkus '74
1985 Members of Lloyd & Dorothy Grinager Family:
   Howard L. Grinager '70
   Christine Grinager Howard '71
   Eric C. Grinager '75
   John F. Grinager '75
   Don L. Grinager '84

Distinguished Alumni

Outstanding Service to Alma Mater

To an alumnus in recognition of outstanding service to Dakota Wesleyan University.

Past Recipients:

1958	Harmon Brown '22
1959	Mae Kelly '28
1960	Robert H. Wagner '36
1961	Harland H. Allen c'13
1962	L.G. Druschel '16
1963	Robert Parkinson '33
1964	Charles L. Calkins '17
1965	Philip Laurson '07
1966	Alta Witzel Sloan '11
1967	Underwood W. Hilton '29
1968	Marjorie Thurston '22
1969	Robert Plastow '55
1970	Matthew D. '12 & Loretta Smith
1971	Jean Weston '21
1972	Jack Leach '28
1973	Kenneth Sherman '31
1974	Gordon Fosness '57
1975	Dorothy Nelson '29
1976	Gladys Keyes Ehrstrom '22
1977	Don Swanson '41
1978	Elmer '18 & Anna Reinecke Lushbough '20
1979	Rollie Kelley '49
1980	Bill '50 & Harriet Nelson Houk '50
1981	Frances Blessing Wagner '38
1982	Wayne Williamson '47
1983	Darryl Patten '60
1984	Kent Millard '63
1985	Donald E. Meager '63

Distinguished Alumni

Outstanding Educator

To an alumnus for notable service in the field of education.

Past Recipients:

1978	Dean Berkley '48
1978	Julian Hartt '32
1978	Leonard '50 & Thelma Murphy Herbst '47
1978	Richard '56 & Glennie Trimble Tays '56
1979	Laura Stark Johnson '37
1979	John Wollman '50
1980	Rose Marie Moran '59
1980	Levi Tschetter '63
1981	Adair Callison '50
1981	Halvin Johnson '56
1981	Mary Lou Voigt '73
1982	Members of the E.J. White Family:
	Fern White Andresen c'25
	Russell W. White '31
	Clarion White '34
	Wendell White '37
	Glenn White ex'40
	Robert M. White '47
1983	Paul Carlson '62
1983	Thomas Morris '54
1984	A. Lloyd Piggee '70
1985	Philip Kaye '42
1985	Hugh Piyasena '61

Distinguished Alumni

Distinguished Service to College and State

To a South Dakota alumnus who has made noteworthy contributions to the betterment of both Dakota Wesleyan University and South Dakota.

Past Recipients:

1963	J. William Kaye '21
1964	Merrill Coddington '24
1965	Elgie Coacher '25
1966	Carl Quarnberg ex'06
1967	Raymond Y. Chapman '26
1968	Parry S. Nelson '48
1969	Oscar Howe '52
1970	Forest Gaetze '37
1971	Don Barnhart '57
1972	Clare (Cy) Holgate '28
1973	Sally Bauman '34
1974	Maxine Schrader Wiseman '31
1975	Paul '40 & Esther Blessing Rollins '40
1976	Grace Sherwood Monroe c'22
1977	Dave Evans '35
1978	Helen Franks Bumgardner '29
1979	Dale V. Andersen '38
1980	Donald Klarup '53
1981	Daniel J. Moran '62
1982	Vernon Ashley '54
1983	Richard Ward '65
1984	Harry Ernst '25
1985	Dean P. Sorenson ex'61

Distinguished Alumni

DWU Athletic Hall of Fame

Richard "Bud" Dougherty	Coach '18-'27	1977
Glenn "Slick" Draisey	Athlete '46	1977
Gordon Fosness	Athlete/Coach '57	1977
Kenneth Harkness	Athlete '20	1977
M.A. "Babe" Hoellwarth	Athlete '35	1977
Mark Payne	Athlete '15	1977
Matthew D. Smith	Contributor '12	1977
Clarence Beck	Athlete '25	1978
Elton Byre	Athlete '60	1978
Bruce Crockett	Athlete '48	1978
Glenn Phillips	Athlete '35	1978
George Smith	Athlete '57	1978
Galvin Walker	Athlete '23	1978
Don Rose	Athlete '50	1979
Jerry Walton	Athlete '56	1979
Zach Wipf	Athlete '24	1979
Vern Fairfield	Athlete '28	1979
Doug Barber	Athlete '50	1980
Fred "Jake" Beier	Athlete '34	1980
Art Fishbeck	Athlete '32	1980
Erv Herther	Athlete '25	1980
Earl Hilton	Athlete '51	1980
Harvey Schaefer	Athlete '61	1980
Lyle Nelson	Athlete '26	1981
Cliff Mackey	Athlete '35	1981
Russell Smith	Athlete '55	1981
Wayne Thue	Athlete '66	1981
Ken Barnhart	Athlete '29	1982
LaVerne Hubbard	Athlete '32	1982
Gordon Zapp	Coach '63 - '68	1982
Frank Lochridge	Athlete '50	1982
Ron Wiblemo	Athlete '53	1983
Clare "Cy" Holgate	Athlete '28	1983
Doug Barth	Athlete '68	1983
Jim Nolt	Athlete '63	1983
Stuart Landersman	Athlete '53	1984
Elgie Boyd Coacher	Athlete '25	1984
Tom Billars	Athlete '68	1984
Charles Summers	Athlete '46	1984
Robert McCardle	Coach '49 - '54	1984
Vernon "Stretch" Belcher	Athlete '50	1985
Sidney Horman	Athlete '33	1985
Forest "Bing" Gaetze	Athlete '37	1985
Don Screes	Athlete '60	1985

Index

Academic departments, structure of, 11-12,36,37-38, 47-48, 55-57, 69, 95-97, 102
Academy (*see also* Preparatory), 36, 37, 42, 99, 124, 128
Accreditation, 37, 47, 91, 96, 97
    North Central Association of Colleges and Secondary Schools, 33, 35, 37, 91
    State Department of Public Instruction, 37
    nursing program, 96
Adkinson, A.W., 8-9
Afro-American Center, 100
Agenda for Excellence, 94, 105
Allen Hall, 67, 81, 83
Allen, Harland, 67, 129, 133
Alumni organizations, 20, 46, 72, 78
American Indian studies, 97
Andrews, Bishop Edward G., 3, 4
Art, 12, 53, 57, 96, 98, 123, 124, 127
Articles of Incorporation, 5, 11, 119
Asbury, Bishop Francis, 2
Athletic conferences and national organizations, 18, 44, 60, 75, 103
    Dakota-Iowa Conference, 60
    Minnesota-Dakota Conference, 44
    National Association of Intercollegiate Athletics (NAIA), 103
    South Dakota College Conference, 60
    South Dakota Intercollegiate Athletic Conference (SDIAC), 44, 60
    South Dakota Intercollegiate Athletic Association (SDIAA), 18
    South Dakota Intercollegiate Conference, 60, 103
Athletic Hall of Fame, 103, 136
Athletic organizations at DWU, 18
    Athletic Board, 46, 72
    Mitchell Athletic Association, 46
    "W" Club, 46, 73
    Women's Recreational Association, 75
    Young Women's Athletic Association, 18
Athletics, 15, 16, 17, 18, 20, 32, 44, 45, 46, 50, 54, 60, 61, 72, 103, 104
    Archery, 46
    Baseball, 18, 28, 45, 75, 103
    Basketball, 18, 29, 30, 41, 45, 58, 60, 75, 76, 87, 95, 101, 103, 104
    Cross country, 103
    Field hockey, 76
    Football, 19, 41, 45, 53, 60, 75, 76, 103
        "Powder puff", 76
    Golf, 75
    Hiking, 46
    Hockey, 41, 46

Soccer, 75
Swimming, 29, 35, 45, 75, 87, 94
Tennis, 45, 95, 103
Track, 18, 19, 29, 35, 45, 58, 60, 95, 103
Volleyball, 29, 46, 76, 87, 95, 103
Wrestling, 73, 75
Attention Center, 97

Baccalaureate service, 15, 67, 106
Backus, Reno, 44
Bailey, Howard, 73, 74
Barr-Hartung, Fay, 98
Bauman, Melvin, 57
Beck, Frank and Bessie, 44, 131
Beddow, James B., 25, 93, 94, 95, 98, 99, 106, 119, 129
Beddow, Jean, 98, 106
Beecher, Alvah, 39, 56
Belding, Lester, 61
Black Hills College, 32, 72
Black Hills Mission, 32
Blodgett, P.L., 19
Blue and White Book, 43, 59
Blue and White Day, 29, 40, 41, 53, 57, 58, 65, 66, 67, 103
Board of Education (Methodist), 2, 12, 22, 66, 98, 107, 111
Board of Trustees (formerly Board of Directors), 1, 4, 5, 8, 9, 16, 31, 32, 33, 34,
    35, 36, 37, 48, 49, 50, 51, 52, 54, 55, 64, 65, 73, 74, 89, 90, 93, 94, 101, 107, 109,
    119, 121
Boarding clubs, 34, 39, 40
    Cosmo Club, 34
Bobb, Byron A., 15, 119, 129
Boulton, Bishop Edwin C., 106
Bowdle, A.M., 3, 21, 22
Bowles, Henry, 17
Brother, My Song, 70
Brown, Harmon, 50, 121, 133
Brumbaugh, Jesse, 17, 19
Brush, William, 4, 5, 7, 8, 9, 13, 15, 22, 24, 110, 119
Burnham, Linda, 98, 100
Burr, Leona, 44
Bush Foundation, 104, 130
Business department (*see also* Commercial Department), 11, 12, 32, 69, 82, 96

Calkins, Charles L., 64, 133
Campus buildings:
    Allen Hall, 67, 81, 83
    Century Memorial Hall, 10, 11, 15, 20 22, 26, 32
    Chapel/fine arts building, 92, 94
    Christen Family Recreation/Wellness Center, 87, 95

138

College Hall, 8, 11, 13, 14, 19, 23, 28, 33, 36, 40, 41, 53, 58, 60, 64, 65, 66, 67, 72, 76, 78, 79, 80, 99, 107

Dayton Hall, 54, 65, 66, 67, 68, 76, 81, 101

Fredericks' Place (President's Home), 89

Graham Hall, 10, 32, 35, 38, 39, 44, 50, 51, 53, 58, 59, 64, 66, 99, 101

Merrill Memorial Hall, 4, 7, 8, 21, 26, 66, 67, 78, 110

Morrow Gymnasium, 29, 35, 45, 51, 76, 81, 87, 94

Music Hall, 27, 32, 81, 95

Phillips Hall, 5

Prexy Lodge (Music Hall), 27, 32, 44, 52

Rollins Campus Center, Gordon and Elsie, 67, 71, 80, 81, 84, 93, 98, 99, 100, 101, 106

Science Hall, 28, 33, 34, 54, 65, 68, 81, 82, 93, 95

Smith Hall, 40, 66, 80, 81, 82, 88, 93

Stout Hall, 29, 35-36, 81

Campus carillon, 93

Campus organizations:

Afro-American Center, 100

Aqua Sharks, 72

Ben Gals, 72

Circle K, 72, 76

Cosmopolitan Club, 72

Dolphin Club, 46

Inter-Society Council, 46

Oyate Ho Waste, 100

Recreational Sports Board, 101

Student Activities Board, 101

Student Association, 20, 46, 101

"W" Club, 46, 72

Wesleyannes, 100

Writers' Club, 59

Campus minister, 44, 73, 74, 102

Carhart, Ernest A., 57

Carhart, Florence, 44

Carhart, Raymond and Edith, 44

Carhart, Walter and Ethel, 44

Case, Senator Francis, 42, 46, 65, 67, 70, 93

Case, Leland D., 53, 70, 131

Case, Myrle G., 70

Centennial observances, 94, 106

Center for Frontier Studies, 70

Central Dakota University, 4, 5

Century Memorial Hall, 10, 11, 15, 20, 22, 26, 32

Chandler, Augusta L., 12

Chapel, 7, 14, 15, 28, 33, 40, 44, 58, 59, 60, 73, 74, 88, 93, 94, 100, 102

compulsory attendance, 73, 74, 100

services, 59, 73, 74, 102

Roman Catholic, 73

Chapel/fine arts building, 92, 94
Chapman, Madge Corwin, 14, 26
Chenoweth, Richard, 70
Christen, Paul and Donna, 87, 94-95, 129, 130
Christen, Philip and Ruby, 95, 129
Christen Family Recreation/Wellness Center, 87, 95
Claggett, Evalyn Sougstad, 98
Clark, Badger, 15, 65, 70
Class memorials, 40, 86
Collections, library, 15, 70
    Badger Clark, 15, 70
    Jennewein, 70
    Jedediah Smith, 70
    Preacher Smith, 70
    Senator Francis Case Archives, 70
College Department, 11, 37, 123, 124, 127
    Classical course, 8, 12, 111
    Scientific course, 11, 111
College Hall, 8, 11, 13, 14, 19, 23, 28, 33, 36, 40, 41, 53, 58, 60, 64, 65, 66, 67, 72, 76, 78, 79, 80, 99, 107
    Fire of 1955, 64, 65, 79
Colleges of Mid-America, 93
Colton, E. T., 17, 20, 131
Commander, Jane Case, 70
Commencement, 8, 15, 16, 51, 67, 91, 93, 106
Commercial Department (*see also* Business Department), 12, 32, 37, 38, 57, 69, 96, 111, 123, 124
Computer network, 70, 99
Comstock, Donna, 57
Corn Palace, 43, 51, 58, 76, 91, 94, 106
Counseling, 99
Cropp, D.B., 19
Culver, Mrs. H.C., 51
Cummerford Corporation, 89, 90
Currens, Maggie, 12

Dakota Conference, 1, 2, 4, 5, 7, 8, 9, 13, 21, 32, 34, 47, 51, 52, 107, 115
Dakota Mission (of the Methodist Episcopal Church), 2, 3, 4
Dakota University, 2, 3, 4, 5, 7, 8, 9, 10, 11, 12, 13, 15, 16, 17, 18, 19, 21, 22, 23, 31, 110
Dakota University and College Alliance, 3, 22, 109
Dakota University Athletic Association, 18
Dakota Wesleyan World, 100
Dakota Wesleyan Forensic Board, 42, 46
Dakota Wesleyan University, name change to, 31-32
Dancing, 14, 41, 51-52
Dayton Hall, 54, 65, 66, 67, 68, 76, 81, 101
Dayton, Grace Bliss, 66, 129

140

Debate (*see also* oratory), 16, 17, 42, 43, 57, 72
Deficit, 21, 55, 90, 91
Degree programs:
    Advanced, 37
    Associate, 96
    Baccalaureate, 38, 96
Dewey, Charles, 71, 129
Dieken, Mel, 70
Doggett, Bruce (Chris Cain), 70, 132
Dougherty, Richard "Bud," 30, 45, 103, 136
Draisey, Glenn, 103, 136
Drama, 16, 39, 42, 43, 56, 65, 70, 96
    Prairie Players, 56
    Productions, 43, 56, 67, 70, 96
Dress codes, 100
Druse, Katherine, 59
Dunbar, Ralph, 57
Duncan, T.A., 8, 9, 18, 22, 121

Early, Jack Jones, 25, 66, 67, 69, 74, 98, 119
Eastman, Fred C. and Mrs., 7
Edge, Joseph H., 25, 52, 54, 119
Educational program, 11-12, 31, 33, 34, 36, 37, 54, 55, 56, 69, 95
    general, 36, 38, 69, 95, 96, 102
Ehrstrom, John, 63
Elocution, 12, 15, 123, 124
Employee compensation and benefits:
    Group health insurance, 64
    Retirement program (TIAA-CREF), 64
    Salaries, 9, 22, 50, 64, 66, 69
        Non-cash equivalents, 50
    Social Security, 64
Endowment, 33, 34, 35, 47, 49, 51, 61, 64, 77, 90, 93, 94, 104, 110, 121, 122
English, 9, 19, 36, 39, 42, 43, 71, 72, 128
Enrollment, 7, 8, 10, 31, 32, 35, 36, 37, 39, 50, 51, 53, 54, 55, 56, 61, 64, 66, 67, 68, 69, 73, 89, 91, 94, 96, 97, 123-126
    impact of war, 35, 39, 53
    post-World War II, 53, 54, 55, 61
    and Eastern recruitment, 68
Exchange program (DWU-Koka Institute), 97
Eyres, Mildred, 71

Faculty degrees, 13, 36, 91
Family Life Conference, 69
Fees, 47, 101
Ferguson, Stuart, 60
Fiftieth anniversary (1935), 50, 51

Films:

    At the Edge, 94

    Brother, My Song, 70

    Candy, 73

Financial assistance, 13, 21, 22, 23, 47, 50, 52, 68, 94, 99, 104

    National Youth Administration (NYA), 50

    Revolving student loan fund, 52

Fires

    College Hall (1955), 64, 65, 79

    Merrill Memorial Hall (1888), 8, 21, 26, 107

First Methodist Church (Mitchell), 8, 16, 60, 65

Forbes, Marie, 71

Forensics, 19, 42, 43, 57, 71, 72, 97

Fosness, Gordon, 75, 103, 104, 133, 136

Founders' Day, 67

Fredericks, Goerge, 89

Fredericks' Place (President's Home), 89

Friends of the Middle Border, 53, 65, 70, 71

Frost, Bernice, 38

Future Teachers of America, 56, 69

Gaetz, Amelia "Billie," 71

Gates, Cliff, 71

Gateway, 72, 78

G.I. Bill of Rights, 53

Gilliland, Clarence V., 32, 34, 37, 120

Girls State, 92

Goering, Orlando, 69

Graduate Department, 37

Graham Hall, 10, 32, 35, 38, 39, 44, 50, 51, 53, 58, 59, 64, 66, 81, 85, 99, 101

Graham, William I., 10, 11, 15, 19, 24, 31, 119

Gramm, Merlin, 97

Grants, 68, 69, 94, 104

    Basic Institutional Development Program (Title III), 98, 104

    Bush Foundation, 104, 130

    National Endowment for the Humanities, 104, 130

Great Depression, 36, 50, 61

Guy, John, 98

Hardy, Clarion DeWitt, 42

Harkness, Kenneth M., 30, 44, 103, 131, 136

Harkness, Marguerite, 44

Harrison, Lawrence "Pops," 68

Hartung, John, 76, 120

Hauser, Gold, 93, 117

Hauser, J.P., 17

Heetland, David, 101

Henson, Thomas D., 71, 95, 120

Hilburn, Samuel, 25, 54, 55, 69, 119
Hills, Loran, 98
History, 9, 12, 19, 32, 34, 36, 39, 53, 57, 71, 96, 98, 128
Hitchcock, Abner E., 4
Hobson, Emory Wilberforce, 32, 38
Hoellwarth, M.A., 103, 136
Holgate, Helen Fishbeck, 39, 56
Home economics (domestic science), 38, 56
Homecoming, 41, 46, 58, 59, 76, 101
    queen and king, 58
Honorary degrees, 15, 35, 66
Honorary societies, national, 72
Houk, Harriet, 71, 133
Houk, William, 93, 133
Howe, Oscar, 57, 135
Hubbard, Faith, 96
Hubbard, LaVerne "Hub," 58, 136
Huddleston, Robert, 25, 68, 89, 90, 98, 119
Hughes, Ethel Johnson, 59
Human services (*see also* social work), 97
Hyde, Melvin W., 50, 55, 120, 131
HYPER (Health, Physical Education and Recreation), 97

Ingham, Septimus W., 1
Initiation, 58
Interim studies, 95, 96

Janes, Arza, 8
Japanese-American Relocation Committee, 53
Jares, Wayne, 71
Jedediah Smith Collection, 70
Jenkins, John Prince, 32, 47, 48
Jennewein, J. Leonard, 53, 65, 68, 70, 71
Jennewein Western Library, 53, 70
Johnson, Margaret, 72, 96
Joint Archives (of DWU and the Annual Conference of the Methodist Church),
    71
Jones, Hilton Ira, 33
Jordan, Grace B., 53
Junior-Senior Banquet, 40, 58

Kaye, J.W., 39, 135
Kaye, Philip, 65, 70, 134
KDWU (radio station), 65
Kerfoot, Samuel Fletcher, 24, 32, 33, 119
Kilstrom, Vera, 71
Knox, Boyd, 90, 93, 119, 129
Knox, Jesse, 55, 71, 120

143

Kohlstedt, Edward D., 24, 35, 36, 47, 119
Koka Women's Institute (Japan), 97
Kudlacek, Milton, 98
Kugel, Elizabeth, 71
Kugel, William F., 69, 70

Lady Tigers, 103
Language, 12, 32, 36, 43, 55, 71, 96, 97
Lardner, James Lawrence, 17, 42
Library (Layne Library), 14, 15, 33, 49, 64, 70, 71, 83, 98, 99, 100
    Center for Frontier Studies, 70
    technology, 70, 99
Leach, John V. "Jack," 71, 129, 133
Lecture series, 44, 68, 75, 106
    Family Life Conference, 69
    Lyceum course, 44
    Stark Lectures, 68, 75, 106
Lee, Myrtle Ray, 12
Leonard, Delores, 69
Literary societies, 7, 14, 15, 16, 17, 20, 41, 42, 46, 58
Lyceum course, 44

Mahoney, C.K., 44
Martin, Jim, 104
Mathematics, 9, 11, 13, 36, 53, 55, 69, 71, 98, 128
Mathieu, David, 97
McGovern, Eleanor, 92
McGovern, George, 57, 70, 72, 92, 93, 106, 131
    Presidential campaign, 71, 92
McGovern Room, 70
McLaird, James, 98
McRae, Roberta, 58
McVay, Winifred, 17
Meals, 13, 22, 39, 71, 84
Memory Lane, 78
Merica, Charles O., 9, 10, 24, 119
Merrill, Bishop S. M., 7, 26
Merrill Memorial Hall, 4, 7, 8, 21, 26, 66, 67, 78, 110
    Fire of 1888, 8, 12, 16, 21, 26, 107
Messer, Bonnie, 90, 97, 98
Messer, Donald, 25, 68, 89, 90, 91, 92, 93, 98, 100, 103, 106, 119
Messer, Joe, 69
Methodist Board of Education, 2, 12, 22, 98, 107, 111
Methodist Crusade for Christ, 52, 115
Methodist Episcopal Church, 1, 2, 4, 5, 7, 12, 32, 54
    Board of Education of, 2, 12, 22
    Dakota Conference of, 1, 2, 4, 5, 7, 8, 13, 18, 21, 32, 34
    Dakota Mission of, 1, 2, 3, 4

144

Methodist Hospital, 38, 60, 96, 100
Millard, Kent, 68, 133
Millard, Minnietta, 93
Miller, Alan, 104
Miller, Lauritz, 20, 119
Miller, Marvin, 98
Miss Wesleyan, 41, 58
Mitchell Village (archeological excavation), 98
Mitchell, David, 98
Morrison, F.E., 41
Morrow, Joseph T. and Florence, 35, 129
Morrow Gymnasium, 29, 35, 45, 51, 76, 81, 87, 94
    Men's dormitory addition (Stout Hall), 29, 35-36, 81
Moyer, Carlotta, 7
Moyer, E.T., 7
Murray, O.E., 8, 20
Music Hall, 27, 32, 81, 95
Music, School of, 28, 32, 33, 36, 38, 39, 43, 52, 56, 69, 96
Musical groups:
    Band, 27, 38, 69
    Choral, 38, 56, 67, 70, 106
    Orchestra, 38

National Endowment for the Humanities, 104, 130
Native American students, 97, 100
    Oyate Ho Waste, 100
Nelson, Dale, 96
Nelson, Lyle, 103, 136
Nicholson, Thomas, 11, 24, 27, 31, 32, 36, 119
Nielsen, Paul, 103
Noble, Dell, 9
Non-traditional students, 95, 97, 100
Normal Department, 11, 12, 13, 37, 38, 123, 124, 127
North Central Association of Colleges and Secondary Schools, 33, 35, 37, 91
Nursing program, 38, 69, 96, 128
    Black Hills satellite program, 96

Oratory (*see also* debate), 16, 42, 43, 57, 73, 96
Ordway, 3, 4, 5, 109
Osterhaus, Martin, 2
Otis, Ken, 57
Oyate Ho Waste, 100

Panty raid, 59
Pardee, I.N., 3, 5, 109, 119
Parkin, Giles, 8
Parkinson, Jerry, 58
Parks, Ron, 103

145

Patten, Darryl, 96, 97, 133
Payne, Mark, 45, 103, 136
Pennington, Bob, 71
Phillips Hall, 5
Phillips, O. A., 4, 5
Phreno Cosmian (student newspaper), 20, 37, 43, 59, 68, 72, 100, 111
Pi Kappa Delta, 42, 72
Pitcher, Horton, 8
Political activities, 39, 46, 73, 92, 97
Political science, 19, 98
Pow wow, 101
Prairie Players, 56
Prairie Wind, 59, 72, 100
Pranks, 15, 40, 58
Preacher Smith Collection, 70
Preparatory Department (high school), 11, 16, 20, 23, 37, 111, 123
Preschool, 98
Presidential Scholarships, 105
President's home, 27, 32, 52, 89
Prexy Lodge (Music Hall), 27, 32, 44, 52
Programs, pre-professional, 69, 97
Prohibition, 39
Publications:
    Blue and White Book, 43, 59
    Dakota Wesleyan World, 100
    Phreno Cosmian, 20, 37, 43, 59, 68, 72, 100, 111
    Prairie Wind, 59, 72, 100
    Tiger Tribune, 100
    Tumbleweed, 20, 59, 72, 100
    University Herald, 20

Randall, F. Dwain "Doc," 105
Randall Scholars Program, 104-105
"Rec," the, 58, 76
Religion in Life Week, 75
Religious affiliations, student, 73, 75, 102
Religious organizations, 17, 43, 44, 59, 75, 101
    Brothers and Sisters in Christ (BASIC), 101
    Catholic, 75, 101
    Chrysalis, 101
    Fellowship of Christian Athletes, 75, 101
    Kappa Chi, 59, 75
    Life and Service Club, 43
    Lutheran Students, 101
    Methodist Student Movement, 59, 60, 75
    Outreach groups, 17, 102
    Oxford Club, 43
    Religious Life Council, 59, 74, 101

Student Volunteer Band, 43, 44, 59
    Young Men's Christian Association (YMCA), 16, 17, 39, 43, 44, 59, 102, 107
    Young Women's Christian Association (YWCA), 16, 17, 18, 43, 44, 59, 102
Reno, P.O., 8
Residence hall fees, 22, 50
Residence hall regulations, 72, 100
Residence halls:
    Allen Hall, 67, 83
    Dayton Hall, 54, 65, 66, 67, 68, 76, 81, 101
    Graham Hall, 10, 32, 35, 38, 39, 44, 50, 51, 53, 58, 59, 64, 66, 81, 85, 99, 101
    Phillips Hall, 5
    Stout Hall, 29, 35-36
Rich, Chester, 57, 69, 120
Rietz, Harold, 103
Rising, Lloyd, 42
Roadman, Earl Allen, 24, 36, 49, 50, 51, 57, 119
Robbie, Joe, 94, 129
Rogers, Emily, 8
Rollins Campus Center, Gordon and Elsie, 67, 71, 80, 81, 84, 93, 98, 99, 100, 101, 106
Rollins, Barbara, 72
Rollins, Gordon, 55, 80, 90, 98, 99, 121, 129
Ronald, W.R., 57
Ruth, Bob, 100

Scallin, Fred, 103, 129
Schaeffer, Carrie, 41
Schermerhorn, W.D., 24, 34, 35, 44, 119
School colors (blue and white), 17
Schuerle, Paul, 69
Science, 12, 33, 36, 38, 55, 70, 82, 98
Science Hall, 28, 33, 34, 54, 65, 68, 81, 82, 93, 95
Scotchman, the, 59
Seaman, Walter Grant, 24, 33, 34, 55, 119
Seaton, J.L., 32
Senator Francis Case Archives, 70
Seventy-fifth anniversary (1960), 64, 66, 72, 96
Shandorf, Fred and Mary Cass, 88, 93
Shandorf Chapel (aka "Upper Room"), 60, 88, 93
Shanton, J., 7, 12
Shepherd, A.C., 17, 20
Shepherd, W.S., 20
Sherman, Kenneth and Marian, 93, 129, 130, 133
    Chapel/theatre, 93
    Endowed scholarships, 105
Shurtleff, M.A., 12
Sioux quartzite, 7, 110
Skinner, May, 8

Smith, Judge Frank, 22
Smith Hall, 40, 66, 80, 81, 82, 88, 93
Smith, Loretta, 44, 57, 63, 66, 80, 133
Smith, Matthew D., 25, 44, 55, 57, 63, 64, 65, 66, 67, 80, 103, 119, 120, 133, 136
Social work, 97
Sougstad, Ed, 71
Sougstad, Mike, 66
South Dakota Conference (of the United Methodist Church), 1, 104, 119, 130
South Dakota Foundation of Private Colleges, 64
South Dakota Intercollegiate Forensics Association, 42
South Dakota Intercollegiate Oratorical Society, 16
Special Services, 99
Speech, 12, 16, 19, 42, 72, 92, 106
Stanford, Senator Leland, 21, 129
Stark, Franklin C., 68, 106, 129, 131
Stark Lectures, 68, 75, 106
Starr, Esther, 12
Starr, Herbert and Gyda, 95
State Board of Education, 12
Stout Hall, 29, 35-36, 81
Stout, Levi Asa, 9, 10, 13, 22, 36, 56
Student Army Training Corps, 34
Student government, 34, 46, 52
    Student Senate, 46, 72, 75, 100, 101
    Women's Self-Government Association, 46
Sunderman, Marilyn, 93
Sweetland, Leon, 25, 51, 52, 114, 119

Tatina, Robert, 98
Teacher preparation and training (Department of Education), 8, 11, 12, 13, 21,
    37, 38, 55, 56, 96
    Collegiate Department, 37
    Graduate Department, 37
    Normal Department, 12, 13, 21, 37, 123, 124, 127
    practice teaching, 69
Territorial Board of Education, 12
Thanksgiving Day football, 19, 45
Thompson, Helen, 71
TIAA-CREF, 64
Tiger Lair, 76
Tiger Tribune, 100
Tigers, 45, 53, 60, 75, 103, 104
Title III (Basic Institutional Development Program), 98, 104
Title IX (Equal Opportunity), 103
Tooke, McKendree, 22, 109, 119
Trimble, Helen, 98, 120
Tuition, 22, 37, 47, 49, 50, 51, 94, 122
Tull, Clyde, 43

Tumbleweed, 20, 59, 72, 100
Turchen, Lesta, 98
Turchen, Michael, 98

United Methodist Church, 1, 89, 90, 91, 106, 119
 Board of Education of, 66, 98, 107, 111
  University Senate of, 12, 111
 college's relationship with, 1, 5, 12, 18, 21, 32, 35, 47, 51, 52, 75, 89, 91, 93, 107
 South Dakota Conference of, 1, 104, 119, 130
United Methodist Scholarship, 104
University Herald, 20
University High School (*see also* Academy, Preparatory), 37
Upper Room, 60, 88

Van, Amber, 44, 131
van Benthysen, S.D., 32
Van Kirk, James, 39
Van Kirk, Katherine, 39
Veglahn, Donald, 106
Vietnam War, 73, 91, 95
Von Eye, Rochelle, 98

Wagner, Robert, 25, 65, 66, 90, 106, 119, 133
Walker, Galvin, 103, 136
Walton, Wendell, 55
Washington Birthday Banquet, 14, 40, 58
Way, John F., 47, 52, 121
Way, Walter, 47
Weinkauf, Mary, 72
Weir, Samuel, 32, 34, 120
Weller, Sam, 103
Weston, Jean, 71, 84, 133
White, Florence, 71
Whitfield, Wilmot, 3, 109, 119
Wieczorek, Todd, 103
Wieting, C. Maurice, 43
Williams, Thomas, 56
Williamson, Wayne, 59, 69, 133
Wilterdink, Duane, 102
Windle, Beulah, 8
Wing, Mary, 70
Wingert, Joe, 71
Wingfield, Frank, 71
Wintemute, Virginia "Ginger," 97
Wipf, Zack, 103, 136
Woolsey, Mary, 69, 71
World War I, 31, 34, 39, 45, 54

149

World War II, 30, 53, 54, 56, 61, 71, 78
Wright, Michael, 98

YMCA-YWCA Student Movement (*see also* Young Men's Christian Association,
    Young Women's Christian Association), 17
Young, Bradley, 65, 119
Young Men's Christian Association (YMCA), 16, 17, 39, 43, 44, 59, 102, 107
Young Women's Christian Association (YWCA), 16, 17, 18, 43, 44, 59, 102

Zapp, Gordon, 75, 136